dream home

*The art of building a sanctuary
for modern, healthy living*

LUKE DAVIES

Re^think

First published in Great Britain in 2025
by Rethink Press (www.rethinkpress.com)

© Copyright Luke Davies

All rights reserved. No part of this publication may be reproduced, stored in or introduced into a retrieval system, or transmitted, in any form, or by any means (electronic, mechanical, photocopying, recording or otherwise) without the prior written permission of the publisher.

The right of Luke Davies to be identified as the author of this work has been asserted by him in accordance with the Copyright, Designs and Patents Act 1988.

This book is sold subject to the condition that it shall not, by way of trade or otherwise, be lent, resold, hired out, or otherwise circulated without the publisher's prior consent in any form of binding or cover other than that in which it is published and without a similar condition including this condition being imposed on the subsequent purchaser.

To Janenna, Bella and Roy

This book is dedicated to you, with boundless gratitude for the love, patience, and unwavering support you've shown as I embarked on this writing journey. I hope these pages not only inspire you to chase your own dreams but also remind you that the seemingly impossible can become reality. Thank you for being the light that guides me, always.

Contents

Introduction   1
    My journey   3
    How this book will help   5

PART ONE   Getting Started   11

1   The Habitat Hierarchy   13
    Maslow's Hierarchy of Needs   14
    Our needs for the built environment   16
    House, home and dream home   21
    Summary   23

2   Do Your Home-work   25
    Set up a recording system   26
    Set a regular date night   27
    Clarify your priorities   28
    Balancing energy efficiency and budget   32

The full immersion experience	32
The Dream Home Journal	34
Summary	38

PART TWO The Six Elements — 39

3 Purpose — 41

Goals	42
Location	45
Activities	47
Your life stage	48
Your dream home values	49
Summary	52

4 Landscape — 53

Micro-environment	54
Local regulations	62
Site services	66
Orientation	66
Summary	72

5 Function — 73

Home habits	74
Floor area size	75
Flow	76
Efficient layouts	82

Housework and storage	85
Livable housing	90
Relationships	91
Summary	94

6 Feeling — 95

The five senses	96
Moods	100
Materials and texture	103
Lighting	105
Colour	107
Fittings, fixtures and finishes	108
Biophilic design	111
Volume, space and scale	112
Summary	114

7 Health — 115

When buildings make us sick	116
Water	117
Air	123
Temperature	127
Light	127
Electromagnetic fields	129
Wellbeing	130
Summary	136

8	**Technology**	**137**
	Building standards and the National Construction Code	139
	The building envelope	141
	Passivhaus Standard	150
	Energy use and energy-saving techniques	156
	Smart homes	159
	Summary	162
9	**Our Home, Planet Earth**	**165**
	Human impact	166
	Zero waste habitat	171
	Sustainability plus regenerative design	182
	Other design principles explained	184
	Summary	188

PART THREE Understanding The Industry   189

10	**Home Construction Options**	**191**
	Certainty versus flexibility	191
	An existing house	192
	Off-the-plan	193
	Standard custom	193
	Architectural	194
	On-site or off-site?	196

Design and construction 197
Summary 198

11 Building A Team — 199
Roles on a construction project 200
Finding your team 210
Questions to ask 214
Summary 216

12 Aligned Build Collaboration — 217
Conventional tendering 218
The ABC Method 221
Summary 228

13 Budgeting Project Costs — 229
The myth of the square-metre rate 230
How to do a project feasibility study 231
Project costs 233
The Four Ss 237
Counting costs 242
Summary 247

14 The Aligned Dream Home — 249
The BuildPrint 250
Project milestones 253
Summary 258

Conclusion	**259**
Notes	**263**
Acknowledgements	**271**
The Author	**273**

Introduction

Designing and building your own home is the adventure of a lifetime. It's the opportunity to create a space that's perfectly aligned with your aspirations, your needs and your dream lifestyle.

Everything starts with design. Beyond offering the functional benefits of a space tailored to your requirements, a well-designed home can align perfectly with your chosen landscape, improve your health and wellbeing, provide a safe place to connect with family and friends, help you form good habits and make space for your creative pursuits, improve your impact on the environment and give you an unbeatable sense of pride and fulfilment.

My company has worked with dozens of clients to achieve these results – people with design and construction (D&C) budgets ranging from modest to multimillion-dollar. Typically, our clients have searched for an existing home to meet their needs but they just haven't been able to find a place that feels 'right', a house that truly feels like home, so they begin to think about designing their dream home. Sometimes people come to us for advice on buying land. Sometimes they have already purchased a block they love – whether it's deep in the bush with no power, water or sewage connection or on a suburban block within convenient reach of community facilities.

Increasingly, our clients are interested in the impact their home will have on their health and the health of the planet. They want to know how to build to lower their environmental impact and how to use clever design and technology to minimise their energy use.

People who are looking to build their own home are often daunted by three main problems. First, they feel overwhelmed at the thought of starting a home design project. Designing a home is a project with 1,001 moving parts. When you begin, you don't know what you don't know. Each decision unpacks more complexity, and the wrong decision can lead to delays, cost escalations, resentment, conflict and waste. Building a dream home can quickly become overwhelming, chaotic and a straight-up bad experience.

Second, they're concerned about the potential for budget blowouts – and for good reason. Custom-designed building projects are notorious for running over time and over budget. As soon as you stray from the repetitive-production path, you're in uncharted and uncosted territory. For most construction projects, the trade-off for flexible design is budget blowouts, with poor planning, miscommunication, delayed decision-making and incomplete documentation leading to costly mistakes.

Finally, they're worried about quality and not being happy with the end result. In most builds, the devil is in the detail. Vague and unresolved plans leave builders and trades making decisions that can take the project far off-track. Without clearly understanding the vision for the project, tradies are forced to take their best guesses. More often than not it goes wrong, and the homeowner must decide whether to fix it or live with it.

My journey

I began my career as a carpenter and joiner. Since 2009 I have been building architectural homes with a commitment to quality building practices. An architectural home, also known as an architect-designed home, is a home specifically planned and created by an architect. A custom home is a one-of-a-kind house that is designed for a specific client and for a particular location. This could be designed by a building designer or an architect.

In 2012 my construction company began winning awards for the quality of our builds, and we've won many. Some of our more recent awards include the Housing Industry Association (HIA) Tasmanian Home of the Year, the GreenSmart Sustainable Home of the Year and three-time winner of the Tasmanian Master Builder, Residential Builder of the Year and Master Builder Sustainable Home of the Year, Australia 2024.

At some point I realised that no matter how high the standards of my construction, I had no control over the calibre of the design or how it complemented the site or the needs of the owners. I was also working with plans developed long before I came to a project as the builder. Often they lacked detail or contained inaccuracies and impractical features. Filling in the gaps caused delays, budget blowouts and wasteful changes, which frequently created unnecessary stress for everyone involved.

I knew that the only way to improve this process was for the builder and the architect to work closely together from the start, so in 2014 my team began to work with clients to *design* homes as well as build them. I now have an architecture firm founded on collaboration and working with quality-focused builders to deliver high-quality, unique, healthy dream homes – a simple and practical idea we call the ABC Method (Aligned Build Collaboration). It allows me

INTRODUCTION

to build the homes I love and promote better health for my clients and for the planet.

This structured approach means that each and every component of a home design is systematically considered from the start, not on the fly, replacing uncertainty and overwhelm with a feeling of control and confidence, and solving the three problems outlined above. This process of planning the project properly is crucial to taking out the surprises. By exploring as many of the design decisions and iterations as possible while they are still on paper when mistakes are relatively cheap, you can calculate an accurate construction quote and time frame and reduce the chance of changes during construction, which are the number one cause of budget blowouts on architectural home construction projects.

The process reduces miscommunication and eliminates guesswork, enabling the construction team to deliver exceptional quality. It is based on a collaborative approach that brings the architect, builder and key experts together from the design stage to gain a deep understanding of client requirements and specifications. I have learned that construction projects don't go wrong, they start wrong.

How this book will help

In *Dream Home*, I will outline exactly how you can implement this system with your dream home team, no matter where you are in the world. Although my experience has been gained here in Tasmania and Australia, the practices I talk about are relevant anywhere. This is a practical book that will get you scribbling and designing. It will help shape your ideas and fine-tune your thinking.

The Six Elements of a Dream Home[1] is a comprehensive analysis tool to evaluate the relationship between a home, its environment and the people who will live there. By analysing your needs in the six areas of purpose, landscape, function, feeling, health and technology, you will gain a deeper understanding of your requirements. The Six Elements encourage you to examine aspects of your design needs and lifestyle that you may never have considered. It's the basis for a truly responsive design and the perfect foundation from which to brief your architect.

In this book, I'll include exercises which will gradually build your understanding of your design requirements. By the end of the process, you'll be able to approach your architect and builder with a much more nuanced description of your vision, and the ability to communicate it confidently. You'll have a heightened alarm system in the event that your project starts to head off-track, because it's not just about capturing your needs in a design that's in perfect harmony with your lifestyle and your landscape; you also need to realise your dream through a huge construction project involving dozens of people and thousands of small decisions. There are countless opportunities for mistakes. I'll also include case studies that show both where others have got it right and where they have learned from their mistakes.

Building a dream home is an enormous undertaking and it should never be entered into lightly. A custom-build home has the potential to be a terrible experience. It can drag out for years, blow your budget and cause tension in relationships with your family, your design and construction team and your neighbours. A poorly designed home can have a negative environmental impact and carries the potential to make you and your family dangerously ill.

Homeowners need to know about, and ask for, the highest standards in energy efficiency and healthy home principles when designing and building their homes. You will never be fulfilled living in your dream home unless it has been designed and personalised around all aspects of your life. If you think it's all about having new products or fittings and stone benchtops, you've missed the point. It is more than that: it's about the fundamental elements of design and the way that design is personalised to you and your site, and you can't just go to any old architect or builder and achieve this. You have to follow the right process with the right experienced team.

A critical element of the process outlined in *Dream Home* is documented decision-making. In a conventional architectural build, many design decisions are left until the construction phase, leaving open a huge potential for budget overruns. In our system, decisions are documented in the design phase – from the flooring material to the tapware selections. This means the project can be accurately costed from the start. It also reduces waste and the expense of making endless changes while building, which can leave everyone, including the architect, the builder and the homeowner, feeling disgruntled and resentful.

My company's process brings the architect and builder together to work with clients from the first design meeting. This keeps everyone in the loop and drastically reduces the chance for miscommunication.

Information is power, and in *Dream Home* I've shared the methods and equations we use to realistically cost a project. I provide full details of the consultants and professionals who will need to be involved in your project. Equipped with this information, you'll be in a far better position to engage with your team on the fine details of design decisions and their impact on the budget.

Our signature methodology, the Six Elements of a Dream Home and the ABC Method, enables clients to get the design they want and move into their dream homes on time and with confidence around their budgets. For people implementing these methods, this

INTRODUCTION

is absolutely the norm – and it is accessible to you through the pages of this book. If you too would like to renovate, extend or build your dream home on time and on budget, let's get started.

PART ONE
GETTING STARTED

According to the Australian government, Australians spend 90% or more of their time indoors.[2] Whether it's where you work, go to school and live, it's safe to say the built environment makes a substantial contribution to your quality of life and the way your life is shaped.

The design process I follow with my clients doesn't include only the usual elements associated with design – the look and feel – but also covers the end-to-end experience, including working with their team, the design and construction process and living in their home. Designing a dream home, therefore, cannot simply mean designing a building; it must be designing the person's experience with the building, which in return creates a greater quality of life. This takes a significant amount of research, self-reflection and thinking deeply about design, which I've encapsulated in the Six Elements of a Dream Home.

We'll look at the Six Elements in Part II, but to get you started let's examine some of the principles that underpin the system and begin documenting some of the priorities and requirements that will feed into your design.

1
The Habitat Hierarchy

Human beings love beautiful buildings. From the cosy allure of a beaten bush cabin to the grandeur of a historic cathedral or the daring design of a modern art gallery, we love incredible architecture because we instinctively understand that the built environment has a profound effect on our outlook and wellbeing.

The place that has the greatest impact of all is, naturally, where we spend most of our time – our home environment. One of the keys to a successful, creative, balanced, inspiring, healthy and happy life is to understand that our quality of life can be better or worse based on the building we live in. Our homes have an enormous impact on the state of our mental and physical wellbeing, our daily stress levels and our relationships with both our loved ones and the natural ecosystems around us.

Understanding this before you start your home design process will lead to making radically different design decisions. Your home can be an extraordinary sanctuary that will recharge you, inspire you and replenish you, or it can be a joyless space that drains your energy and leaves you feeling unmotivated, disorganised, frustrated and sometimes even physically ill.

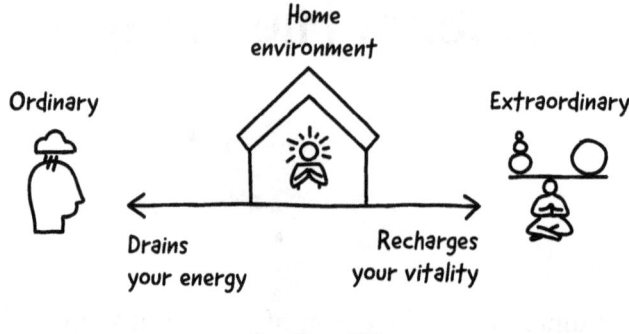

Quality of life

The good news is that there is a systematic way to design an extraordinary home that will create a better quality of life, so in this chapter we'll examine what we need from a home. We'll look at Maslow's famous Hierarchy of Needs and I'll introduce you to my system for applying Maslow's ideas to home design: the Habitat Hierarchy.[3]

Maslow's Hierarchy of Needs

Psychologist Abraham Maslow developed a 'theory of human motivation' known as Maslow's Hierarchy of Needs.[4] It describes the five basic human needs from the most elementary to the most complex, in this order:

1. **Physiological needs:** Air, food, water, shelter
2. **Security needs:** Safety for yourself and your family
3. **Belongingness needs:** Social connection with family and friends
4. **Esteem needs:** Aesthetics, creativity, moods, luxuries
5. **Self-actualisation needs:** Being aware of yourself as well as others and helping others and the planet

The pinnacle of the pyramid (self-actualisation) represents the culmination and execution of the five needs – living to our fullest potential and becoming who we truly are.

This basic framework of Maslow's hierarchy captures a profound truth about human existence. It helps answer the fundamental questions that underpin our lives, such as: 'What do we want from life?', 'What makes us happy?', 'How do we make decisions to ensure we are progressing towards the goals that matter to us?'

Our needs for the built environment

The Habitat Hierarchy adapts Maslow's work for the constructed environment. It's a tool I use to clarify the role that living environments play in our lives. It helps define the way dream homes can produce a different life for the occupant, rather than merely being a simple provision of shelter.

The Habitat Hierarchy is organised in a pyramid structure that maps Maslow's hierarchy. Once we satisfy the first need, we move up through the levels of the pyramid and seek to satisfy the next need until all five needs are satisfied. The desire to move up the pyramid is one key reason we feel the urge to move into a better home or renovate our current home – it is a matter of matching our developing stages of consciousness with our living environment, thereby satisfying our subconscious desires.

Starting from the base of the pyramid, the levels are as follows:

1. **Shelter:** Basic shelter that offers some protection from the elements
2. **Safety:** A space that provides a feeling of safety
3. **Connection:** A space where you feel a sense of connection with yourself, your family and friends – graduating from a house to a home

THE HABITAT HIERARCHY

4. **Pride:** A unique space that is a reflection of your style, personality and social status – your home is purposefully built around your rituals, habits and the moods you want to create

5. **Fulfilment:** A conscious environment that is in harmony with nature and considers the health of the planet – this is your sanctuary, a space to be connected and mindful and to live an extraordinary life

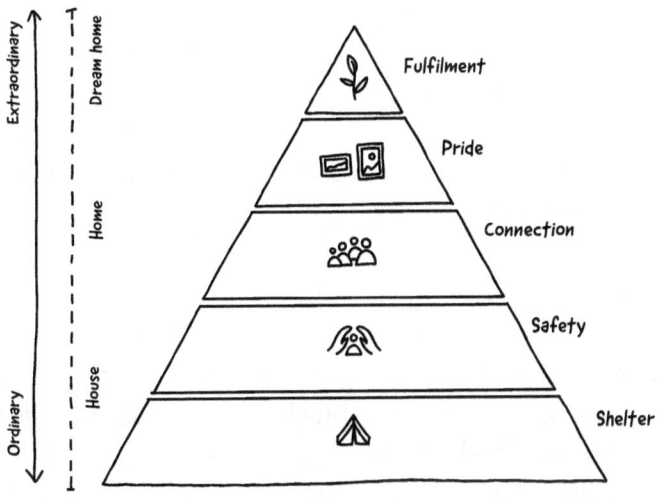

The Habitat Hierarchy

From the most basic to the most bespoke, a home design has the potential to meet human needs for basic shelter right through to fulfilment. Most home designs, however, cater only to the lower rungs on this pyramid.

DREAM HOME

My life provides a great example of the Habitat Hierarchy and how you can move steadily upwards from basic shelter to fulfilment.

When I was a kid, Mum and Dad were dairy farmers. We moved around a lot, living on different farming properties in rural Tasmania, which gets bitterly cold in winter. By the time I was fourteen, I had lived in twelve different houses. Usually, these houses were the second house on an established property and some of them were pretty run-down. I remember one of the houses we lived in was pulled down after we moved out, because no one else was willing to live in it. This house fulfilled only the lowest level of the Habitat Hierarchy – it was a basic shelter with no feeling of permanence or security.

I grew up in bedrooms smelling like mould, with cold night air leaking in through the aged timber window frames and no insulation in the walls or ceiling. My parents blocked rat holes, plugged leaks, scrubbed and painted surfaces to provide us with *shelter* and *safety* – the bottom two levels of the Habitat Hierarchy.

The situation wasn't great, but it sparked my passion for building. I wanted to build better houses for my family to live in. Once I learned how to build, in my teens, the first thing I did was renovate my nan's house, where I was living at the time of my building apprenticeship. I wanted to improve the house for

Nan. The kitchen, dining room and lounge were all squashed into one tiny room. While Nan was away on holiday, I pulled out a wall, added an extension with new windows and door, put in a new kitchen and built a deck. I wanted more than shelter and safety; I wanted a living space that would comfortably allow family and friends to enjoy coming to Nan's house. By renovating these rooms I achieved the level of *connection*, a space we could comfortably share with friends and family.

Once I met Janenna, who became my wife, we decided to build our first house together. We worked over six months after work and on weekends. We did everything: the concrete, the framing, the roofing, the insulation, the plastering, the tiling, the joinery, the painting and the rendering. I can still remember, on the first night we stayed there, the feeling of *pride* I had in building our customised home, the way we wanted it and with my own two hands. It was small and basic, but it still has a special place in my heart as my first home.

From then on, I knew I wanted to be always building houses. Since that first house, I've built another home for my family and many homes for other people – more than a hundred of them. As my experience in building dream homes grew, my curiosity, ideas and capacity for innovation developed. Right now, Janenna and I are building our dream home. We've purchased 17 acres and we're currently building a three-bedroom home to Passivhaus Standard – a benchmark for high-quality building I will discuss in Chapter 8. Our kids are still young, ten and twelve (and love building with their dad), and as we build we are thinking about their future needs as well.

Our site attracts northern sun and has stunning views at each end of the home. We built full-height glass walls to maximise these views and foster a connection with nature. We wanted our build to have reduced carbon emissions, so we used timber for the whole house, and it will be self-sufficient with water, waste water and solar power. We will put in food gardens and revegetate the block with native trees. We'll also have mechanical ventilation with a heat recovery system that brings filtered fresh air in and takes stale air out while exchanging the heat in the air. There's space for our morning rituals – our yoga and exercises – and there's an outdoor sauna and bath.

These days, my home is at a much higher level on the Habitat Hierarchy than those run-down houses where I grew up. My focus is on health – fresh air, sunlight, restful sleep and natural materials. In all aspects of the design, Janenna and I have considered the holistic needs of our family to create a home that is our sanctuary, a space to be connected, that is energising and doesn't consume fossil fuel to operate. A home that, in turn, will bring us *fulfilment*.

House, home and dream home

I group dwellings into three categories based on the Habitat Hierarchy.

A **house** fulfils the needs of only the lower rungs of the Habitat Hierarchy. It is often a standard-issue design which provides shelter and a feeling of safety and security, but little more. In fact, sometimes these buildings can harm your health in what's known as sick building syndrome (SBS), which we'll discuss in Chapter 7, suck your daily energy and affect your physical, mental and emotional wellbeing.

To progress up the pyramid, a house must meet the needs of the occupant in more complex ways. A **home** is characterised as a customised space designed for connection with others that reflects your individual style and values and instils a sense of pride in you, functions how you want, makes *you* healthier, wows your friends and transforms the way you feel each day.

Reaching the pinnacle of the pyramid requires far deeper engagement to work out the perfect balance between nature and building and what will be enough to support the needs, interests, health, wellbeing and creative pursuits of the people who will live in it. People who live in a **dream home** experience a deep sense of fulfilment through connection with their families, improved health and wellbeing, higher energy levels, better habits and a conscious, low-impact and low-waste relationship with the natural environment.

A dream home can be a tiny house or a mansion. The size of your home doesn't have anything to do with the fulfilment you receive from it. We all have different ideas about what is enough for us and what size and style our homes should be; however, every building should be designed and constructed to reach as close to the top of the Habitat Hierarchy pyramid as possible. It gives us a target to aim for.

Understanding the importance of reaching the pinnacle of the pyramid is pivotal in developing the Six Elements of a Dream Home, which comprehensively identifies and measures how well your home fulfils the six fundamental design elements.

DREAM HOME-WORK

Reflect on the houses you have lived in and the Habitat Hierarchy. Can you see a connection?

Consider whether your home is draining your energy or recharging your vitality.

Clarify whether you feel like moving house, renovating your house or building a dream home.

Work out where on the Habitat Hierarchy you feel your current home fits.

Think about how this chapter has made you think differently about renovating or building.

Summary

In this chapter we've explored the Habitat Hierarchy, which is a way to apply Maslow's well-known Hierarchy of Needs to your home environment. The higher your home is on the Habitat Hierarchy, the more of your human needs are being fulfilled in your home environment.

Thinking about your home design in terms of how the Habitat Hierarchy works provides useful insight into how well it meets not only your practical requirements but also your social, psychological and even spiritual needs. Later in the book, I'll introduce you to a practical model for incorporating all these needs into your home design in a systematic way.

2
Do Your Home-work

The journey of creating your dream home is in three main phases: Phase 1 is preparation (home-work and selecting your team), Phase 2 is designing and Phase 3 is building. Each phase has a specific process. Use this book as the tool to help you complete Phase 1.

Precision should be the foundation of every project, and the first step in the home design process is to do your research into both your external inspirations and your internal values, desires and needs. In this chapter we'll begin the brainstorming process with some exercises and activities, and we'll set up systems for you to keep a record of your thinking as you work though the exercises in the chapters to come.

Sometimes this kind of planning can add complexity to your design, but mostly it simplifies things. You might even find after doing the exercises that you don't need all the features you thought you did – a tiny home might be enough to meet your needs – or you might find that an off-grid, self-sustaining home is what's important to you.

Set up a recording system

Start collecting and keeping your ideas. For example, if you enter a building and you like the way the light falls, make a note. If you visit a friend's home and it has a great indoor/outdoor space for the kids to play, grab a measuring tape and make a note. Gather all these notes in one place. You can keep a notebook, use voice memos in your phone or set up a folder, either electronically or in an old-fashioned scrapbook. This will be the place to store your notes, photos and responses to the exercises we'll cover in this book, along with everything else that goes into designing a dream home. If you want a structured hard copy, you can use the Dream Home Journal – I talk about this later in the chapter.

You may already be collecting visual inspirations, eg on Pinterest. This can be a great resource for communicating ideas to your design and construction team. If you're going to use Pinterest, I recommend setting up your board with the rooms you want in your home.

DO YOUR HOME-WORK

Try not to overdo it. You can add as many images as you like, but by the time you are ready to show this board to your designer and builder you want no more than ten images for each room and to have an idea of the specific thing you love in each image. We all come across many sources of inspiration in our daily lives, often when we're offline. Buildings are physical. The best way to experience them – and to analyse what works and what doesn't – is to enter the space, not look at pictures online. It's important to keep a record of these lived experiences in spaces that inspire you.

There are journals, worksheets, checklists and reports to help you on my website, many of which I will signpost you to as you work through the book: **www.lukedavies.co**

Set a regular date night

Long before you involve an architect or builder, you and your loved ones – or anyone who will be sharing the house with you – should be on the same page about what you want and why.

Janenna and I find we need to arrange a time and place to discuss these things. In other words, we set a date night. We spend an hour or so brainstorming or planning, usually starting with one of the lists below. We find that we get down most of the items on a list in one session, and then we'll get the rest over the following few weeks.

Schedule in time to plan your dream home properly, as rushed conversations tend to end in miscommunication. To fully consider your home design you need dedicated time to ponder, discuss and make decisions without distractions. Scheduling dream home date nights, even if just for you, and putting them in your calendar will make them real.

If you find it hard to put what you like into words, try starting with what you don't like. Janenna and I agree on what we don't want and this limits us to the things we do want, bringing us closer to the end result.

Clarify your priorities

Your priorities are the basis of the decisions you make. It's vital to clarify and articulate them so that you can brief your design and construction team effectively. This can save a lot of wasted time, money and frustration.

Your priorities will come into play if you need to make hard decisions. For example, is it more important to take an extra week to fit the antique wooden doors or to meet the project deadline? Different individuals will answer this question differently, and your project will run much more smoothly if your design and construction team understand where your priorities lie.

> **EXERCISE: Personal values list**
>
> You may already have your own clear set of values. If you haven't thought about this before, have a go at answering the following questions. You may have multiple answers – identify answers that are similar and group them together.
>
> If you study your calendar and bank statement, they will tell you what you value.
>
> 1. What do you spend your money on?
> 2. How do you spend most of your time?
> 3. How do you fill your current space?
> 4. What do you most often talk about to others?
> 5. What inspires you and gives you energy?
> 6. What topics do you love to read about or research?
> 7. What do you find yourself thinking about the most?

> **EXERCISE: Project priorities list**
>
> Use your values list to help decide on your project priorities.
>
> 1. In construction, in what order would you prioritise quality, time and budget?
> 2. What is the maximum budget that would make you feel uncomfortable?

3. What is the maximum time that would be too long to wait for your dream home?
4. How important is it for you to work with an architect and builder who share your values and vision?
5. Are you willing to compromise on certain elements of your dream home to stay within budget or meet the deadline?
6. How important is it for you to use environmentally friendly and sustainable materials in your home's construction?
7. Would you prioritise local suppliers and materials over imported ones, even if it impacts the cost or timeline?
8. How involved do you want to be in the decision-making process throughout the construction?
9. How important is it for your home to be low-maintenance and easy to manage in the long run?
10. Are you willing to invest in energy-efficient features that may have a higher upfront cost but save money over time?

EXAMPLE: Priorities list

1. We would always choose quality over time, we would choose budget over time, we are not in a rush, we just want to get it right and how we want it. We value quality of materials, workmanship and the finished product.

2. Our budget varies depending on the design, but exceeding AU$1.8 million would make us uncomfortable.
3. Ideally we want our move-in date to be in two-and-a-half years.
4. It's extremely important to align our values and vision with our team.
5. We are willing to compromise on non-essential elements and listen to experienced explanations.
6. It's important to prioritise environmentally friendly materials.
7. We prefer local suppliers if feasible, but would have to weigh up the impacts on quality, cost and the timeline.
8. We would rather get everything right in the planning phase and let the builders do their work with only moderate involvement through the construction phase.
9. We want to reduce ongoing energy and operational costs by investing in better building processes.
10. We want to make decisions based on healthy products and good indoor air quality.
11. We want to live in sun and natural light.
12. We want to keep warm and feel comfortable all year round whatever the weather.

Balancing energy efficiency and budget

Many dream of a home that's kind to the planet and their wallet, minimising environmental impact while offering long-term cost savings through energy efficiency. However, high-performance building practices and sustainable materials often come with a higher upfront cost, potentially leading to tough choices.

The key is open communication and understanding your priorities. Work closely with your architect and builder to explore options and make informed decisions that balance your values and budget. Prioritise your energy efficiency goals, explore cost-effective solutions, and consider the long-term value of sustainable features. By collaborating with your team, you can create a home that reflects your aspirations while staying within a realistic budget. Every step towards energy efficiency benefits both the planet and your wallet.

The full immersion experience

There's no better way to get a feel for what you like and to fuel your creative thinking than to experience an inspiring home in person. The best way to do that is to stay for a few days.

If you need an excuse to stay in an amazing Airbnb for a couple of nights, I am giving you permission.

Go splurge on an incredible location and property for the full immersion experience. Get inspired. You can repeat this step a few times if you must! There's no monopoly on ideas. Just because someone else has done it, that doesn't mean you can't do it as well.

CASE STUDY: Portugal

A few years ago, I travelled to Portugal with my family. We didn't have any specific plans, we just cruised up the coast for three weeks from the Algarve to Porto. On the way, we used the Airbnb app to find some beautiful homes to stay in while we holidayed.

Our aim was to find inspiring homes. As a result, we ended up travelling a long way off the main tourist route. One of the homes was amazing.

It was built in rugged countryside. There was an amazing outdoor pool surrounded by lush green lawns, there were stunning indoor-outdoor connections and lots of natural materials, and the place had a wonderful energy. We immersed ourselves in the home and its design. I studied the design, the construction and the quality, how things had been done and why they had been done. We watched the sun come up and experienced how the house performed through the day, understanding which rooms received light and at what times. The experience of sleeping in the rooms and using the shower and the fittings was powerful, and the house was inspiring in itself. There were beautiful nooks where I could sit and write. I kept a journal about how the house made me feel and recorded the ideas I had while staying there, and I took lots of photos – all of which reinforced my sense of how much our homes can affect our state of mind and our quality of life.

That house in Portugal had a big impact on the way I'm designing my current home and the ideas I bring to designing other people's homes. In fact, it was in this house that Janenna and I used the tools in the book to draw up the briefs we gave to the architect who designed our current dream home.

Since our trip to Portugal, I've stayed in many inspiring places around the world, and I actively seek them out to open my mind, open my soul and open my heart. Some of these are expensive places to stay, but the value to me of experiencing the architecture of someone else's home is worth it, which is what I tell my wife and accountant. Some of my best memories are anchored to the memory of a building and the experience I had at the time. That's the power of the built environment. When it is good it leaves a lasting impression: great buildings create emotion, and emotion is what creates memories you never forget.

The Dream Home Journal

The Dream Home Journal is your guide to gathering ideas and preparing for your meetings with your architect and builder. By following specific prompts and answering probing questions, you can use the journal to capture your vision and ensure you provide all the necessary information to achieve the best results when designing and building your dream home. By guiding you to avoid common pitfalls, this tool helps prevent projects from going off-track due to lack of knowledge or asking the wrong questions. Remember, the key lies in asking the right questions to receive the right answers and create your perfect home.

The Dream Home Journal includes multiple worksheets and checklists, including a Needs and Wants List, Project Priorities, Love and Frustration List, Habits, Rooms planner, Evoking Emotion, Project feasibility and a space for practical details. With all this information in one place, you'll have a reference you can use to capture your thinking and share with your dream team.

You can obtain a copy of the journal on my website, **www.lukedavies.co/dreamhomejournal**.

Needs and Wants List

This is useful in outlining the specific things you must have in your home and the things you would like to have. It's an invaluable tool for your architect to use in understanding you and your project. Again, keep it somewhere that's easy to access in your daily life.

If you are planning your dream home with another person, then it's good to do this exercise separately and then cross-reference your answers together. I have had a few long silences and awkward laughs in design meetings when a couple had spoken about a certain design need or want for the first time and realised they wanted different things.

> **EXERCISE: Make a love and frustration list**
>
> A great place to start defining the features of your dream home is to look at what works and what doesn't work in your *current* home or other homes where you have taken notice.
>
> The Love and Frustration List is a simple but powerful exercise. Simply draw a line down the centre of a sheet of paper so you have two columns. At the top of the left column write 'What I love most about my current home' and on the right side write 'What frustrates me about my current home'. There is a template for this is included in the Dream Home Journal.
>
> Keep this list somewhere handy. Every time you think of something you love or that frustrates you about your home, add it to the list. As you think more deeply about building your dream home, you will begin to notice things about your current home that you hadn't noticed before.
>
> The Love and Frustration List captures all the details you would otherwise forget when the time comes to meet your architect and builder. In the frustration column you can also add things you hate to see in a home even it's not in your current home, to make sure your architect avoids them.

For example, when I was designing my home, I added:

- **Love:** I love the way I can soak up the morning sun and enjoy my cup of tea in the kitchen. I love being able to lie in the bath and gaze out the window over the farmland. I love natural material and finishes.
- **Frustration:** I don't like the way the rubbish bin in the kitchen works. I don't like the clutter in the doorway as I enter, tripping over school bags, shoes and handbags. There's no clear spot for car keys. I don't like how the shower goes cold when someone turns on another tap. I don't like chrome tapware. I don't like lots of grout in the shower that needs cleaning.

Dream Home Evaluation

The best way to create a sound plan is to define your starting point. To assist with this, I have built a simple online evaluation tool to highlight the strengths and weaknesses of your current home: the Dream Home Evaluation.

Complete the evaluation at **www.lukedavies.co/ dreamhomeevaluation**. It takes about five minutes and you receive a free evaluation report that benchmarks your current home using the Six Elements of a Dream Home.

The Ready to Build Quiz is a valuable tool designed to help you assess your preparedness for building your dream home. This comprehensive quiz covers essential aspects such as cost research, finding skilled builders and architects, understanding local regulations, defining your budget, considering environmental impact and more. By answering these crucial questions, you can gain valuable insights into your readiness for starting the building process and identify areas that may require further attention or research. You'll find it at www.lukedavies.co/readytobuildquiz.

Summary

The exercises in this chapter will set a strong foundation for your dream home design. By now you will have set up a recording system and the Dream Home Journal, clarified your project priorities and made a Love and Frustration List, set a regular date night to discuss your design, planned a few full immersion experiences and completed the Dream Home Evaluation and the Ready to Build Quiz.

At this point you should have a clearer understanding of your priorities and design values, but how do you translate these values into a design? Now we're ready to look at the Six Elements of a Dream Home.

PART TWO
THE SIX ELEMENTS

The Six Elements of a Dream Home is a system devised to evaluate and design a building, considering the ways it interacts with the environment and the people who spend time there. The mistake most people make is designing the home well in only two or three of these elements; for a true dream home, you need to address all of the Six Elements.

The Six Elements are:

1. **Purpose:** The reason why you are building
2. **Landscape:** The specifications of your site
3. **Function:** The right floor plan
4. **Feeling:** A place that feels like home and creates the right vibe

5. **Health:** A healthy and comfortable living environment

6. **Technology:** The correct building method and materials

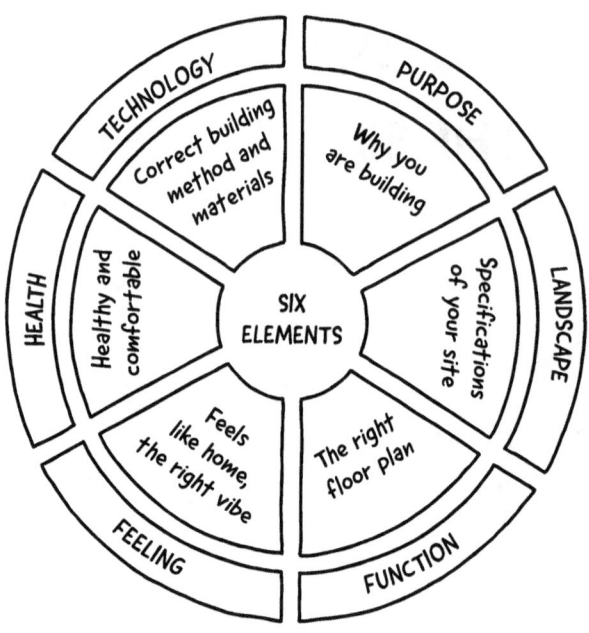

The Six Elements

The Six Elements can be used in any D&C scenario, from an office to a school or accommodation, but I wrote this book specifically to apply these elements to a dream home. In the following chapters, we'll take an in-depth look at each one.

3
Purpose

Why do you want to build a dream home? A home is so much more than just a roof over your head. Your home must align with your vision for your future. It must help you achieve your goals for life, include space for all the activities you love, match your phase of life and cater to the needs of each person who will reside in the space.

In this chapter we'll look at the purpose of your home and each of its sub-branches: goals, location, activities, stage of life, and your dream home values.

Goals

Many people begin the home design journey because they cannot find an existing house on the market that feels like 'home'. For these people, designing their own home is a pathway to achieving their desired quality of life.

Some people have set a goal of building to flip their home and make a profit in the real-estate market. Others want to build a home with sections they can use for extra income by renting them out on sites like Airbnb. Choosing to build a home means you can put your budget towards the areas that are important to you.

> **EXERCISE: Why do i want to build?**
>
> Ask yourself the question 'Why do I want to build?' and make a list of your answers. For example, before I started working on the dream home I'm currently building for myself and my family, I asked the question and here's what I came up with:
>
> - I really value quality and I couldn't find an existing home that lived up to my standards.
> - I wanted an energy-efficient home that was warm and cheap to heat/ run. I couldn't find this in an existing home.
> - I wanted a building that would be resistant to climate change to protect my family from fluctuating weather events.

- I wanted the floorplan and layout to suit the way I wanted to live.
- I wanted new fittings and finishes.
- I wanted to spend my money on the things I cared about and valued.
- I wanted to build a family home that would be around long after me.
- I was not worried about resale for this home.
- I wanted a healthy home and couldn't trust how other homes had been built.
- I wanted my home to be carbon-neutral and provide me with the fulfilment of knowing that I am living in a home that doesn't use fossil fuel, such as coal or gas.
- I wanted a home that my kids wanted to stay in and come back to even as they grew older.
- I felt the strong desire to build rather than settle for an existing home that was built to meet some else's needs.
- Once I found out about the Passivhaus Standard of building (see Chapter 7), that became the baseline for the standard of building I wanted to live in.
- I love creating and building, I probably love the building process as much as I enjoy the finished product.

Your goals should guide your design at every stage. They will help you to stay committed and keep you motivated when you hit bumps along the D&C journey.

The best way to think about this aspect of purpose is to relate it back to the Habitat Hierarchy. If you are on a hiking trip and you put up a tent, your motivation for constructing the tent is most likely limited to simple shelter. This works well for an overnight stay in the wilderness, but it would not be ideal for long-term living.

As you move up the pyramid, your motivations become more complex. Once you reach the pinnacle of fulfilment, you're designing a home to improve both your quality of life and the home's impact on the planet. When building for fulfilment, you need to investigate your requirements and values in a holistic way to ensure your design measures up and you don't end up with something that disappoints you.

CASE STUDY: David and Lily

David had a successful medical practice in a small community in Tasmania, but David and Lily decided to move an hour away to Hobart when their children reached high-school age, as it meant their teenage kids would not have to board at school.

The goal for building this home was to provide a home for David and Lily and their two teenagers and this fed into every aspect of the design. The block was chosen for its proximity to the school and sports venues. There were quiet study areas built into each of the kids' bedrooms, and plenty of space for the teenagers, including a downstairs area with a table tennis table where they could make noise without it impacting the rest of the house. They also had their own living area upstairs, with their bedrooms opening onto a shared TV and computer game area, and there was enough bathroom space for everyone. David had a comfortable home office so he could work from home where possible to avoid the commute, and Lily, who was running a busy household, had us design a spacious kitchen, laundry and other work areas.

This family home was designed to cater to one phase in the family's life. It was designed around the need for everyone to have private space, to study hard and to let off steam when necessary. This design suited David and Lily's specific needs; a family with no kids, younger kids or more kids would have created different design needs and different design solutions.

Location

When choosing your site, you must ask some probing questions about what you and your loved ones value most. For example, do you love living close to nature more than the café culture of the inner city? How far are you willing to travel to work, school, the hospital or the supermarket?

Here are some of the factors that feed into your choice of location:

- Aspect (including view, sight lines, sunlight)
- Climate (average weather and weather extremes)

- Proximity to family and friends
- Commute time
- Landscape (nature, city, beach, mountains)
- Access to schools or universities
- Atmosphere (quiet and serene or bustling with energy)
- Access to surrounding facilities (hospitals, gyms, movie theatres)
- Availability of restaurants
- Internet connection

CASE STUDY: My home

I live where I do because I have family and friends in this location. I also love the rural setting and lifestyle. When selecting the building site for my dream home, I had a few specific criteria in mind, related to the way I want to live and feel.

First, I wanted to have space around me. I wanted some land so I could let my children run around like I did when I was growing up on dairy farms. I wanted to grow my own food on that land. I wanted room for a big shed for me to build and tinker with woodworking projects.

Second, I wanted a long view of the horizon to witness sunrises and sunsets. The position of the sun and the way it would intersect with my dream building site was important to me, so I looked for (and found) a site with all-day sun.

Finally, I wanted a view of the mountain that is prominent in our town. All these factors fed into the block of land that we selected.

Activities

Before you meet your architect, start thinking about how you aspire to live in your home and its surrounding landscape.

It's important that your home includes space for the things you and your family value and the things you want to spend time doing. These might include creative pursuits such as painting or making music. They might include recharge spaces to practise meditation or take a bubble bath. You might want a chill-out space to watch a film, play table tennis or a computer game, or spaces where you can host dinner parties, kids' parties or barbies. You might need work spaces where you can set up your home office, fix your car, restore a sideboard or sew a quilt.

On the other hand, there may be activities you'd like to reduce or discourage. For example, you may decide to create spaces that are free of technology, or place TVs and other screens in a separate room so they don't dominate living areas.

Your life stage

Are you building your home to grow a family or to downsize and retire? Is this your first home?

Each life stage has differing requirements for space, safety and accessibility, as well as different capacities for maintenance, cleaning and upkeep. It's well worth considering the life stages yet to come to ensure your home meets your needs well into the future: a dream home. Germans build one home to last them a lifetime; it's a different way to think about building.

You may identify with being in one of the following life stages:

- **Starting out (age eighteen to thirty):** Typically, people are building a first home in this stage of life. They may want to include extra room if they plan to expand their family in the future, or design to extend their home later if the budget is tight.

- **Room for a family (age thirty to fifty):** People in this age group may need to design for the needs of children, including the impact that these needs will have on working areas such as bathrooms, kitchens and laundries.

- **Middle years (age fifty to sixty-five):** In this age group many people are downsizing after children have left home. They may be more focused on hobbies and creative pursuits and build spaces to accommodate them.

- **Later life (age sixty-five plus):** At this stage of life many people have retired and their home must meet their needs for longer periods of the day. Accessibility may also be a consideration; for example, many people choose to build a single-storey home to avoid stairs, or install a lift if the home is two-storey and build so they can age in place.

It's worth considering that our lifespans are expected to lengthen over the coming decades. You could be in your home a lot longer than expected.

Your dream home values

Your home can follow your rules. Decide on a set of values that are the rules and principles everyone who comes into your home follows. For example, we have our core home values written on the fridge so everyone in the house can see clearly what they are. When our kids' behaviour and decisions do align with our home values, we give them kudos. When they do not, we challenge their actions while relating our comments back to one of our core values for the home.

This is what's on the fridge:

> **THE CORE VALUES OF THE DAVIES HOME**
>
> 'Our goal as parents is to simply raise healthy, happy, independent children'
>
> 1. **Freedom:** You have freedom in life to make your own choices and decisions. You are the author of your life. You are free to experiment and to learn the laws of logic and cause and effect.
> 2. **Self-responsibility:** You must take full responsibility for your choices and actions. You do not assign blame or responsibility to anyone else for the choices you make or the actions you take.
> 3. **Mutual respect:** You are free to operate in any way you choose as long as you don't violate the rights of other people around you. You must always treat others with respect, kindness and love.

We all walk past these values every day and we talk about them every night over dinner. We welcome family and friends into our home and expect them to abide by these values as well.

This may not affect your home design; however, your architect might enjoy knowing what dream home values you intend to set.

DREAM HOME-WORK

Write down your *goals* for building your home.

Make a list of all the people who will *use* your home – both as residents and as regular guests. Have you catered to everyone's needs for a safe, comfortable and accessible home?

Think about what your ideal *location* is for your dream home. What site services are important to you?

Make a list of every *activity* that takes place in your home and every activity you wish to take place in your home. Does your home design make space for all of them?

Consider your *current* stage of life and your life stages to come. Will your needs change in the future?

Work out what building standard you want to achieve. In an ideal world I would recommend setting the goal to build to certified Passivhaus Standard.

Overarching purpose statement

Now see if you can distil your purpose down to a few dot points that answer the question: 'Why do you want to build a dream home?' Your answer might be something like 'I want to make a supportive home for my kids in their teenage years so they don't have to leave home', or 'I want to build a home I can live in for the next fifty years and that is on a flat site and close to facilities', or 'I want to get away from the rat race and live off-grid and closer to nature', or 'I want to build a home that will be healthy for my family and the planet'.

Write this statement in your Dream Home Journal.

Summary

The purpose element of your dream home provides a foundation for the other five elements. It looks at your motivation and priorities to ensure your dream home design provides space for each person who will live in it and the activities that are important to them. It considers the surrounding services and amenities of your ideal building site, and takes a look into the future to make sure your dream home continues to serve you for as long as you plan to live in it.

4
Landscape

Every home exists in its own specific setting, which includes the geographic location, topography, climate and terrain. Your home design should respond to the particularities of your site, and you should carefully consider factors such as rainfall, temperature extremes, access issues, the threat of bushfire, flood or wind, the proximity of neighbours and many other factors.

You can rely on your design team to consider these things, but it's imperative to have a basic understanding of the parameters so you can ask the right questions. In this chapter we will consider how your home will sit in the landscape by addressing the following factors: micro-environment, local regulations, site services and orientation.

We'll go on a deep dive into designing for the particulars of the site you have selected. This element has a close relationship with environment-positive construction, as we look at ways to interact positively with the natural environment on the site. The subject of sustainable building is more comprehensively covered in Chapter 9.

Micro-environment

The micro-environment of your site includes the climate, weather, seasons, aspect and terrain. Below are some common micro-environment considerations that can affect your building design.

Climate

Australia has eight different climate zones. The Australian Building Codes Board (ABCB) provides a brief description of each climate zone set out in their National Construction Code (NCC), which is their design and construction provisions for buildings:

- **Climate zone 1:** Hot humid summer, warm winter
- **Climate zone 2:** Warm humid summer, mild winter
- **Climate zone 3:** Hot dry summer, warm winter

- **Climate zone 4:** Hot dry summer, cool winter
- **Climate zone 5:** Warm temperate
- **Climate zone 6:** Mild temperate
- **Climate zone 7:** Cool temperate
- **Climate zone 8:** Alpine

For example, some sites in Tasmania are subject to snow. This impacts the way the roof should be pitched and the engineering in the building, which will need to account for snow loading. It may also change the way you cut and fill and the positioning of driveways so you can access the site easily when it has snowed. It could even affect the construction schedule, as the site may be inaccessible or impractical during the snowy season.

The National Construction Code of Australia makes recommendations for sites subject to snow, strong winds, salt spray, flooding and many other factors. It doesn't hurt to have a conversation with your design team around the issues specific to your site, as wherever you are in the world, there will be factors that need to be considered.

Inside each climate zone there are also microclimates. Sheffield, where I live, is cooler than Hawley Beach where we regularly build. Sheffield is more prone to condensation and heating issues than Hawley Beach because it is 30 kilometres inland. I know locations that frequently have an immensely heavy frost, while some sites in the same area rarely have a frost (if at all). These microclimates are not covered by the ABCB's descriptions; they can be picked up only by asking questions and talking to locals. If you are moving to a new area, or building somewhere like Tasmania where a sunny coastline can be within one hour's drive of a lush rainforest or a barren highland covered in snow, you need your designer to ensure you are designing to align with your microclimate.

Trees

Many people are attracted to sites with beautiful tree cover; however, trees can present the risk of both falling and bushfire, and it can be a heartbreaking decision to remove the features you love about a site.

You don't always have to remove the trees around a house. In some cases, trees can remain right beside a home or even inside a home. If there is any disease or danger from high winds or other factors, however, trees can pose a serious safety risk. It's important to get expert advice about this.

I consulted on a site where a couple had bought a beautiful block with massive gum trees that stood 35 metres high. The trees were one of the features that drew them to the block, but there was nowhere on the block to build a house that wasn't vulnerable to being hit by a falling tree. We realised we'd have to cut down some trees, which was the last thing the couple wanted to do. In this case, though, it was necessary: some of the trees had rot, and these trees were large enough to crush the house and anyone inside it if one *was* to fall.

It's preferable to keep established trees wherever possible, but if there is a danger to the house or you want to let in sunlight, they need to be removed. The danger posed by trees depends on the age and species of tree; some trees are more likely to fall or burn than others.

It's important to think about which trees you want to remove before you build. It costs about three times more to remove a tree once the home is built, as the tree arborists need to work around the building. The cost of getting the labour and equipment to the site is a large part of the overall fee, so it will be cheaper per tree to clear a number of trees than just one or two. The size of the tree can also affect the cost of removal. You should budget for tree removal depending on how many must be cleared and the access to the site.

If you are going to remove a large tree stump from the ground in the same location as where your home is going to be built, it's a good idea to clear the tree stumps three to four months before you begin to build. This allows the ground to reabsorb moisture from where the tree had been extracting it from the ground. There could also be higher ground movement as the ground readjusts to the absence of the tree, which could have an impact on your home's foundations.

Sloping sites

If you have a steep site, you may need to make a big site cut, which has cost implications. These extra costs mean many people are deterred from buying blocks on steep terrain. Due to this cost factor, however, steep sites can oftentimes be cheaper to buy, which can offset the cost of earthworks. There are often great views from steep blocks and the constraints of a steep or awkward block can produce amazing design outcomes. You can sometimes find designers and builders who specialise in steep, tricky sites.

I have seen cases of people buying land and then realising it's in a landslip area, so make sure you find out whether this applies to your site. There are different grades of landslip sites, and these can have a huge effect on what you can build and the cost to build it. Landslip sites have limitations on how much you can dig out of the bank and what type of foundations you can use.

Earthworks

Every site will need earthworks. Usually, the steeper the site the more excavation is involved. There are costs associated with excavation, which include many

LANDSCAPE

factors other than just the labour. For example, the site costs increase if hitting rock, there is awkward access or limited parking.

Nobody can be certain about what is below the ground, and it's one area of a builder's quote that cannot be a fixed price. In my career, I have been lucky to have had only a few jobs out of hundreds to have major cost implications with earthworks.

The excavator you use on your site may range from 1.5 tonnes to 40 tonnes and the hourly rate of these could range from AU$80 to AU$350 per hour.

I went to a site recently and the land was covered in big boulders. The grass wasn't growing over them and you could see the tops of these big rocks sticking out of the ground. I was doing the project feasibility study and I added AU$25,000 for the excavation allowance because I knew we would not be able to excavate the site without hitting those rocks. The people who had just bought the block had not taken this into account.

Drainage

Another issue with sloping sites is drainage. On any site, it's important to look at how water naturally runs on the land. Some blocks are wet, and some blocks drain well by themselves. You need to understand where you can build on the site and whether you have to build your house up so that water will run away from it, not towards it. You can usually tell if the site has water lying in it or wet areas by the type of grass. If it's wet you might see rush-type grass growing in low areas.

Soil type

Soil types have a range of classification – from sandy soil to highly reactive clay soil. This has an enormous impact on your home's concrete footings. For example, if you've got an S site, the slab might be able to be poured straight onto the ground. Sand moves a lot less than clay, which means it doesn't matter as much whether it's wet or dry. Clay soil, however, can move a lot. When it's wet it will expand, and when it's dry it will shrink and crack. Your footing structure and the foundation of the house has to be designed exactly to the soil type. Always find out your soil type as soon as you can in the process. These include:

- **Class A:** Mostly sand and rock; minimal ground movement due to moisture changes
- **Class S:** Slightly reactive clay or silt
- **Class M:** Moderately reactive clay or silt
- **Class H1/H2:** Highly reactive clay
- **Class E:** Extremely reactive clay
- **Class P:** Problematic sites (includes fill, sites with uncontrolled moisture conditions, or significant variation of soil properties across the site)

It's relatively easy for engineers to design the structure above the ground. The challenging part is engineering the foundation so it has minimal movement based on the ground it's built on. Engineers will increase the size of footing and add more steel reinforcements and concrete to account for the soil type and changing ground conditions. There will be more risk of your foundation moving on a P site than an S site and your foundation could then cost tens of thousands of dollars more to construct. It's important to discuss the soil type of your block with your design team, as it will also change the way you need to maintain your home.

Other micro-environment considerations

There are many other issues that could come into play in your particular site. For example, there may be protected animals in your area, or animals – such as wombats or rabbits – who might try to dig into your foundations. There could be termites or insects that can damage the structure of your home. In urban areas, you may need to design for factors such as reducing aircraft noise.

Questions to ask your design team

Questions you should ask your design team about the micro-environment include:

- What climate zone and microclimate zone am I building in?

- What are the climate extremes here?
- What are the NCC guidelines or building codes in the area?
- What is my soil type?
- What is the wind category?
- Will I need to remove any trees?
- Does the building site look wet or dry? (Check in winter if possible.)
- Do I need extensive earthworks?
- Is there a risk of hitting rock?
- Are there any landslip issues?

Local regulations

Local governments have specific requirements in place that may relate to anything from fire preparedness to the colour of your exteriors. You may need to adjust your design due to your proximity to sensitive ecosystems, such as national parks or coastal zones, or to meet the requirements of a heritage listing. There can also be restrictions around the types of buildings you can construct and where you can place them on the site due to zoning or local planning overlays.

For example, if you're building on a rural block or even in a subdivision, the local authority may set a bushfire attack level rating (BAL). The BAL is calculated based on things like the type of vegetation, the slope of your land and the surrounding land. This will affect the construction materials you can use and the distance you can build from the boundaries, which may be different to the usual setback requirements. It's worth looking in to the local requirements because you might find a beautiful block but then discover you're not allowed to build within 50 metres of one of the boundaries. These are the classifications for BAL.

- **BAL LOW:** Insufficient risk to warrant any specific construction requirements, but still some risk
- **BAL 12.5:** Ember attack and radiant heat below 12.5 kilowatts per square metre
- **BAL 19:** Increasing ember attack and windborne debris, radiant heat between 12.5 and 19 kilowatts per square metre
- **BAL 29:** Increasing ember attack and windborne debris, radiant heat between 19 and 29 kilowatts per square metre
- **BAL 40:** Increasing ember attack and windborne debris, radiant heat between 29 and 40 kilowatts per square metre
- **BAL FZ (flame zone):** Exposure to flames from fire front likely, direct exposure to flames, radiant heat and embers from the fire front

Types of local government approvals

There are three types of approvals I work with my local authority before we can build:

- **Development approval** authorises you to build a dwelling on the property. A request for this approval requires a site plan, a floor plan and details of the building elevation; no specific details about structural engineering are required for this permit.

- **A building permit or certificate of likely compliance** authorises you to build a specific building on the site. A request for this approval requires detailed architectural plans and engineering plans.

- **A plumbing permit** authorises you to connect plumbing to a specific building on the site. A request for this approval requires detailed plumbing plans.

Covenants

Covenants are restrictions put in place by a developer. They have nothing to do with the council requirements; rather, they are attached to the title of the block. For example, I recently consulted on a home design project where the owners wanted to build a home of 150 square metres but there was a covenant placed on the subdivision by the developer that required all houses to be a minimum of 200 square metres. The idea was to uphold the real-estate value of the area by ensuring the neighbourhood was composed of large homes. I've also worked on a project where a covenant required all houses in a subdivision to use masonry cladding. My clients wanted to use timber cladding, so we had to go to the developer and get approval from them to relax the covenant on that particular block.

The List

There's a resource in Tasmania called The List,[5] which provides information on every block in the state. It includes planning overlays and titles, and offers services detailing previous sale prices for the property and other information. Resources will vary worldwide, but it's worth checking to see if your local authority has something similar.

Questions to ask your design team

These could include:

- Are there any covenants attached to the land title?
- Are there any planning overlays? What are they?
- What permits will I need?
- What is the BAL?

Site services

Your home will need two kinds of service – services to your home, such as power, water, phone or internet, and services that remove what your home produces, such as storm water, sewerage and rubbish disposal.

If your site does not have services connected, you'll have to connect them or construct them on-site, which means you must budget for this additional cost. Some people are scared of purchasing a block without services, believing the cost of connecting them will be prohibitive; however, if you do your project feasibility study accurately, you can be confident about what to expect. In Chapter 13 there is a breakdown of typical costs.

Orientation

Once you've committed to a site, it pays to undertake a realistic analysis of its advantages and disadvantages. If you have stunning views, for example, it's worth designing windows, outdoor areas and living spaces to take full advantage of them. The best homes are always sympathetic to their landscape. The positioning of your dream home on your building site is critical. It pays to sketch up a site analysis; you could have a go at this or your design team can do this on the site visit.

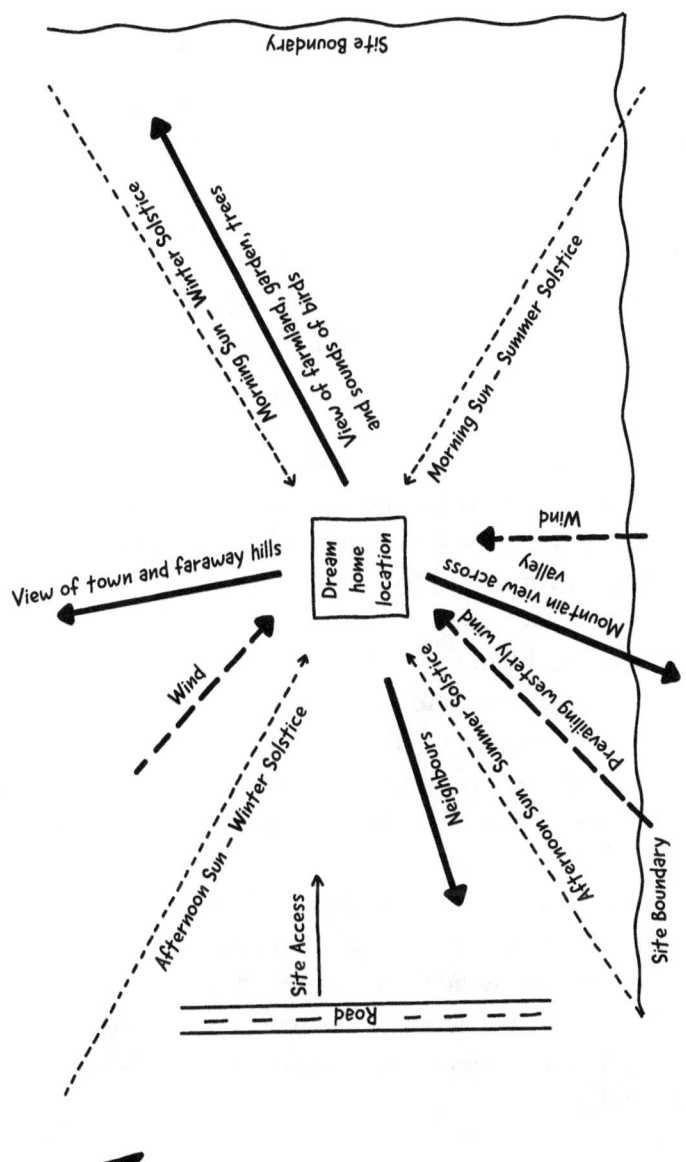

As well as maximising your advantages, smart design can minimise your disadvantages. For example, carefully placed walls can create shelter from high wind, and deep eaves can reduce the effects of soaking rain, maximise winter sun and minimise summer sun. If your block is on a steep incline, you can reduce the cost and impact of substantial earthworks by designing along the contour of the slope. Of course, in colder climates of Australia it's best to orient your home to face north to make the most of the sun.

Make sure to also look up. I have seen houses where no one had bothered to look up during the design phase to check if there were overhead power lines and how close they might be to the building.

The biggest problem I see are homes that are not oriented the right way. Often the garage is a solid wall or there are few or no windows facing north. We use computer software to map the summer and winter solstice when the sun will be at its lowest and at its highest. This then allows us to analyse what effect the sun will have on building design and performance. In Australia we use Bureau of Meteorology data to check prevailing winds for specific building locations. Living in a correctly oriented home makes a world of difference, so make sure you and the design team get this right.

LANDSCAPE

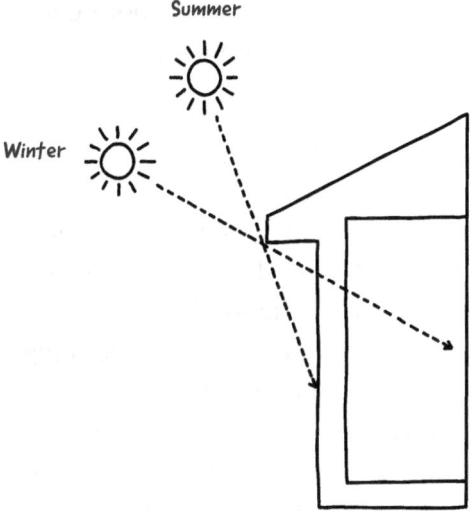

Common diagram

This is a common diagram architects and designers use to show the winter and summer sun angles, and how thermal mass or shading can be used. An often overlooked aspect of the image above is the effect of overshading in the cooler parts of spring and autumn and a lack of consideration of the hot days that are possible in March and October, which bypass the shading elements.

Thermal mass

Thermal mass like concrete or masonry helps stabilise indoor temperatures by absorbing excess heat during warm periods and releasing stored heat during cooler periods. This helps maintain a more consistent and comfortable indoor environment.

Designing for views

I live beneath Mount Roland, which is a stunning peak. It's one of the most photographed mountains in Tasmania, but it is on the south side of town, while the sun is in the north. You can't put all your big windows on the south side to face the view, or you would get limited sunlight into the house. When orienting our new home, I made sure we used the sun and natural light – it creates a nicer, warmer, healthier home to live in.

Landscaping

It's also important to think about how you will landscape your site after your home is built. Most people don't consider this until after they've built their home, but ideally the landscaping and the architecture will work in harmony with each other.

For example, many people plant a lot of trees without considering how big those trees will grow or the shade they will cast on the house, which will have a big impact on solar gains. One solution is to plant deciduous trees so the leaves shade the house in summer but drop away in winter to let the sun through.

Your land's story

Every block of land has its own story and features you can't analyse with data. You have to spend time on the site to hear what the land is telling you. Your architect and builder can be a big help here. Sometimes I will camp on a client's building site to learn more about their special piece of land. If you can't camp on the site then spend time there through the day, take photos of sunrises and sunsets from where you think your house will be located. I have even watched what part of the land the cows like to hangout and lay down in – all this information helps your architect and builder.

DREAM HOME-WORK

Use the Dream Building Site Checklist to help determine how your landscape will affect your dream home design.

Overarching landscape statement

Now see if you can distil your landscape requirements down to a few dot points that answer the question: 'What is the most important feature of my site or ideal site?' It might be something like 'I want an unobstructed view of the ocean', 'I want to catch the winter sun' or 'I want to keep and live among trees'. Consider whether you would be willing to absorb extra costs (eg excavating a steep site) to reach this goal.

Write this statement on your Dream Home Journal.

Summary

The landscape element of the Six Elements takes a detailed look at the specifics of the site where you will build your dream home. You can use the information here while looking at potential building blocks or when you begin to design your site-specific plans.

This element looks at the climate zone and micro-environment of your site, as well as factors like trees, slope and terrain. It looks at local regulations and the availability of services to the site. Finally, it looks at site-specific design and ways to make the most of the features of your site.

5
Function

Most people start the home design journey with a floor plan, and for good reason. You get an instant bird's-eye view of the rooms you want in your home. Your home is the place where you relax and recharge, but it's also a place where you work, cook, clean, wrangle children, do laundry, wash the dog and brush your teeth. Fortunately, smart design and a clever floor plan can make the way you achieve all these things more efficient.

In this chapter we'll consider the impact your home has on your habits, both good and bad. We'll also take a look at designing to maximise the functional effectiveness of your home. We'll cover the following areas: home habits, floor area size, flow, efficient layouts, housework and storage, livable housing and relationships.

Home habits

Human beings are creatures of habit – our lives are a tapestry woven from countless small actions we repeat day after day. These habits, often performed unconsciously, have a profound impact on our happiness, success and overall well-being. We all have habits we are happy about, and others we'd like to change. The good news is, our home design can actively support the creation of positive habits and the reduction of negative ones.

Habits have three elements: a cue, a ritual and a reward.[6] A habit is triggered by a cue; for example, when you wake up in the morning you might immediately reach over and check your socials on your phone, and experience a sense of satisfaction. The cue is waking up, the ritual is checking your phone and the reward is the little dopamine hit from connecting with friends and seeing a like, comment or notification. This pattern creates a habit loop that's hard to break. You have to go back to the cue to break the ritual and the reward. Habits can be changed through discipline or through design.

How can home design help you break this cycle? By creating zero-discipline habits. These work by removing the need for willpower from the habit-breaking or habit-creating equation. For example, in your home design you can place power points a long way from your bed, and charging stations in another room altogether. If you'd like to incorporate more exercise into your daily life, you can position your workout or yoga area in the main living zone, rather than tucking it away at the back of the garage as some home designs do.

Designing a home is your opportunity to think about your habits, and design improved rituals for living.

> **EXERCISE: WRITE DOWN YOUR RITUALS**
>
> Writing down your rituals will give your architect an understanding of how you live so they can make sure your home functions in way that suits you. Spend some time thinking about the following questions:
>
> - What's your perfect morning ritual for a weekday?
> - What's your perfect evening ritual for a weekday?
> - What's your perfect morning ritual for the weekend?
> - What's your perfect evening ritual for the weekend?

Floor area size

A lot of people start the dream home design process thinking about a bigger home than they need. The average house size in Australia is 235.8 square metres, which ranks Australia as having the biggest houses in the world.[7]

Working out the size of the home comes back to creating only rooms you need and ensuring those rooms are the right size. It means running a measuring tape over the rooms in your current home and deciding whether you're happy with the size and how furniture fits into the rooms; for example, the size of bed you're going to put in each bedroom.

Building a home that is too large for your needs will increase your ongoing costs, such as for heating, cooling and maintenance. It will also take longer to clean and can create wasted space, materials and energy, overall having a greater environmental impact.

On the other hand, you may need a big home because you have a large family or entertain a large number of people regularly. You want to be certain it's big enough to be comfortable to live in and that everyone is not living on top of each other.

Flow

Designing for flow in your home means considering the ways you will move between rooms. For example, if your bathroom is at one end of the house and your laundry is at the other, you will have to make a lot of trips between these two rooms carrying dirty laundry.

FUNCTION

When planning and designing a business's work areas, we use a tool called a spaghetti map. We draw a continuous line on a floor plan every time the worker walks to a different area to complete their task. Most people don't fully think about the tools or materials they need to complete the task, or their workspace is not efficiently designed. It's called a spaghetti map because the lines on the page from tracking the walking back and forward, end up looking like a bowl of spaghetti.

Think about your typical movements around your home. Are there ways to increase the efficiency of flow in your design? Here are some examples:

- **Place the access to the garage in the walk-in pantry:** When you come home with bags of heavy groceries, you don't have to carry them far to put them away.

- **Place your home office off the entrance foyer:** You can meet colleagues at the front door without impacting the rest of the family.

- **Place the access to your ensuite in the walk-in wardrobe:** Early risers or night owls can minimise the impact of noise and light on partners who are sleeping.

- **Place outdoor barbecue areas near the kitchen:** You will have easy access to the fridge, sink and kitchen tools.

Zones

The zones of your living space are the broad functional groupings of rooms in your home. Typically, your home will have a mix of the following zones:

- **Approach and circulation zone:** Entry, garage, mudroom, hallway, stairs, porch
- **Live, socialise and cook zone:** Living room, dining room and kitchen, rumpus/family area, outdoor living/dining space, bar, pool, games/play area, courtyard/garden, location of cinema/TV
- **Rest and relax zone:** Bedrooms, nooks, conservatory, loft, nursery, library, prayer room
- **Work, create and exercise zone:** Study, gym, crafts area, workshop
- **Bathe and refresh zone:** Bathroom, ensuite, toilet, outdoor shower, powder room
- **Utility and storage zone:** Storage, laundry and utility rooms, walk-in wardrobe, walk-in pantry, plant room, basement, wine cellar, attic, panic/secret room

Many home designs group wet zones together (such as the kitchen, bathroom and laundry) to create efficiencies in plumbing. You might also ensure that the live, socialise and cook zone is situated to enjoy the best views, while the utility zone might be located at the back of the house. Here are three reasonably compact floor plan design examples.

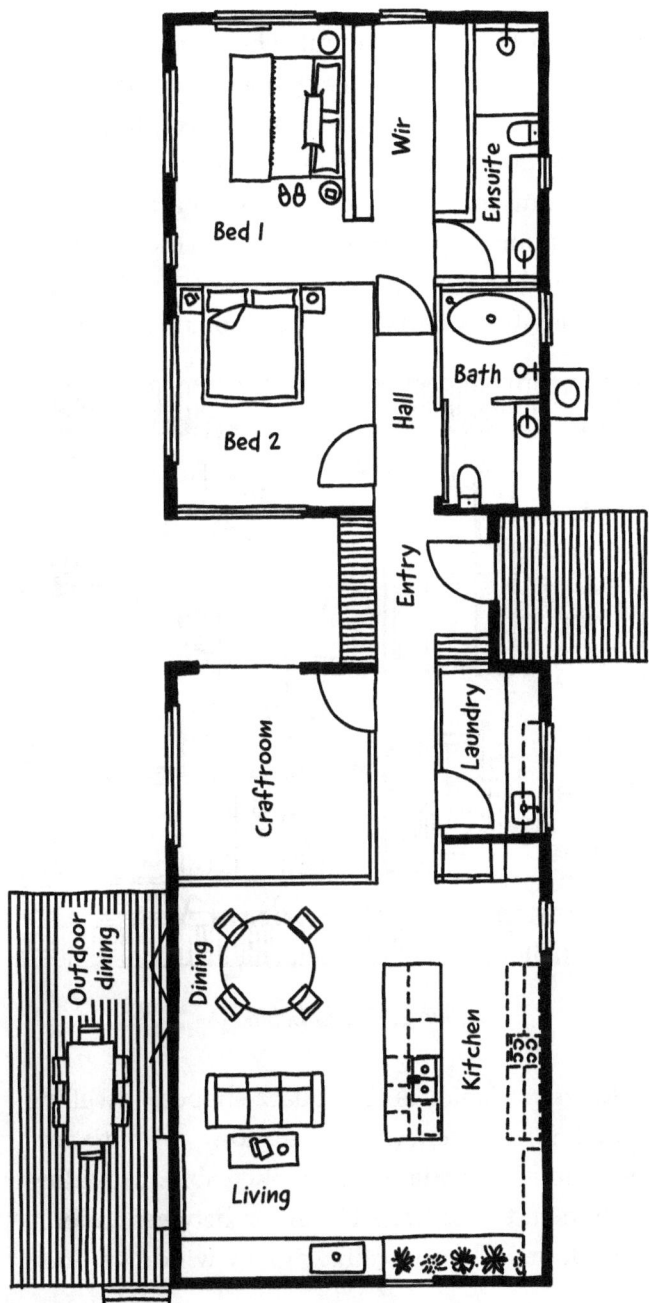

Plan 1: Align Haus

DREAM HOME

The Aligned Haus, a rectangular home with a classic gable roof, features strategically positioned bedrooms to maximise views, while wet areas are grouped at the rear for efficiency. The entryway offers a glimpse into a tranquil internal courtyard, and each bedroom is designed for cross-ventilation. A soaring ceiling in the main living area creates a sense of spaciousness and seamlessly connects to the outdoor alfresco space.

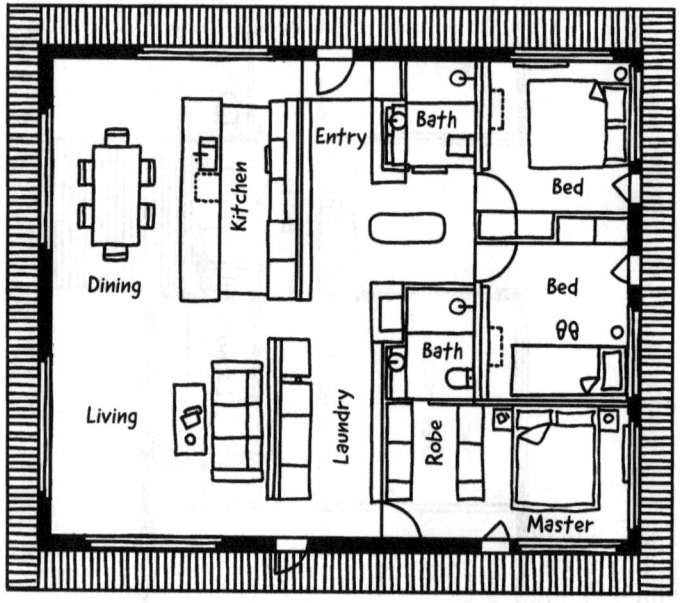

Plan 2: Kaizen Cabin

The Kaizen Cabin is a square-shaped dwelling designed for efficiency and harmony with nature. A continuous veranda encircles the cabin, providing protection and a seamless transition between indoors and outdoors. Floor-to-ceiling glass windows flood the interior with natural light, while the passivhaus Standard ensures optimal energy efficiency and comfort. Inside, three bedrooms are arranged in a row, two sharing a main bathroom and one featuring a private ensuite and walk-in robe. A centrally located kitchen with an expansive island bench encourages family gatherings. A well-organised hallway with ample storage promotes a clutter-free living environment.

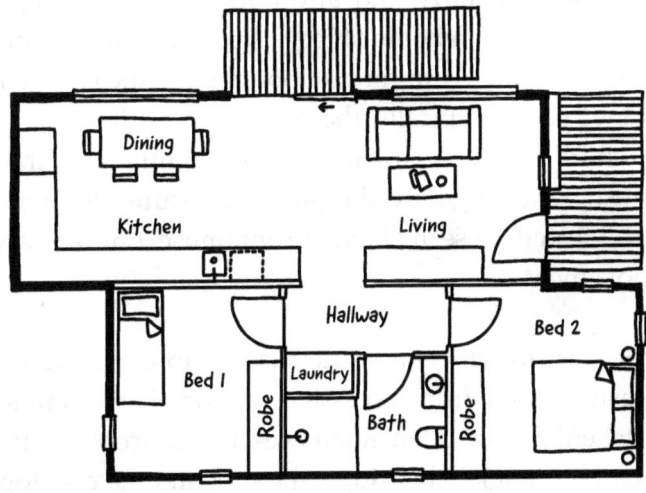

Plan 3: MOD Haus

The MOD Haus embraces modular design with volumetric modules prefabricated off-site for efficiency and precision. This innovative home features two functional bedrooms with a shared bathroom nestled between them, along with a laundry. A separate, spacious volume houses the living, kitchen and dining areas, seamlessly connecting to outdoor spaces and the home's entryway.

Efficient layouts

Along with making it easier to live in your home, efficient layouts are a moral imperative: we owe it to the next generation to be as efficient as possible with the materials we use and the space we take up.

The key workplaces in your home are the kitchen, bathroom, laundry and any other dedicated workspaces, such as a home office, a studio or a workshop. It's important to put careful thought into the layout of these spaces. Typically, these rooms must have space to store supplies and tools conveniently, and they must be intelligently designed to ensure key items are located close to hand to minimise unnecessary movement.

The goal for efficient workspaces is to eliminate the waste caused from excessive motion. For example, kitchen design often references the concept of 'the golden triangle': the fridge, the sink and the cooktop. These are the main working areas of the kitchen and, ideally, they should be placed no further than one step from each other to minimise mess and make cooking more efficient.

There are many possible shapes for a kitchen, such as a galley, a U-shape or an island bench. You might have a butler's pantry with an extra sink, kettle and toaster tucked away. The kitchen is the central meeting place for most modern homes and you should put a lot of thought into designing it.

Placing light switches in sensible locations can make turning lights on and off intuitive for everyone living in the home – although I don't think it would matter where our light switches were positioned, our kids would still forget to turn them off!

Positioning of hot water cylinders and heat pumps/air conditioners should be considered at this stage. You want to make sure the hot water cylinder is as close to your kitchen sink as possible – this is where you want hot water delivered quickly and where you change from hot to cold the most. If you have wall-mounted heat pumps/air conditioners, you want to have the indoor unit in a nice central location and to keep the outdoor unit hidden from the building approach and also away from bedrooms because it will hum during the night.

Feng Shui and Vaastu: Ancient wisdom for modern homes

The flow of energy within a space, whether you call it 'qi' or 'prana', has a tangible impact on our well-being. This concept lies at the heart of ancient practices like Feng Shui and Vaastu, which offer a fascinating perspective on how to create harmonious and balanced living environments.

Feng Shui, a 6,000-year-old Chinese system, guides the arrangement of spaces and objects to promote positive energy flow and enhance well-being. It considers factors like orientation, layout and the placement of furniture and décor to create a home that feels both aesthetically pleasing and energetically balanced.

Vaastu, an ancient Indian architectural philosophy, similarly emphasises aligning buildings with natural forces to promote health, prosperity and overall well-being. It considers elements like the five elements (earth, water, fire, air and space) and their corresponding directions to create a living space that fosters a sense of harmony and connection to the natural world.

While I admit I was initially sceptical of these ancient practices, my perspective shifted as I engaged with clients from diverse cultural backgrounds. Through conversations about home design with a Chinese family and later an Indian family, I gained a deeper appreciation for the profound impact of energy flow on our living spaces. It sparked my interest in exploring how these principles could enhance the well-being and harmony of the homes I build.

Whether you fully embrace these ancient systems or simply draw inspiration from their core principles, incorporating elements of Feng Shui or Vaastu can add a deeper layer of intentionality to your dream home design. It encourages you to think beyond aesthetics and functionality, focusing on how the placement of rooms, furniture and even colours can influence the energy and atmosphere of your living space.

By creating a home that is not only beautiful but also energetically balanced, you can foster a sense of peace, well-being and harmony within your sanctuary.

Housework and storage

When designing your dream home, consider the practicalities of housework and storage. Think about those hard-to-reach corners that gather dust and how you'll manoeuvre around furniture for cleaning. Ensure there's ample space in each room for tasks like changing sheets and vacuuming. Where will you store cleaning supplies and equipment? Will your vacuum cleaner have a dedicated charging station? Is there enough space to fold laundry efficiently? Where are the rubbish bins stored? These seemingly small details can make a big difference in your daily habits.

Having a tidy home helps to create a sanctuary where you feel calm, because a tidy home promotes a tidy mind, creating a sense of calm and well-being. Ample storage is essential for keeping your home organised and clutter-free. Think about all the items you need to store – from sports equipment and seasonal clothes to kitchen appliances and craft supplies. Do you have large items like a piano or a pool table that need a designated space? How will you display your art collection or antique furniture while protecting it from damage?

Smart storage solutions are key, and the 5S system, a simple method for organising, can be a valuable tool in creating a home that truly supports your lifestyle. The 5S system helps you create a designated space for all your belongings and ensures that everything is in its optimal place. This not only makes it easy to find what you need, but also encourages a habit of tidiness. When everyone in the household knows where things belong, it becomes second nature to put them back where they came from. This fosters a sense of order and efficiency, reducing clutter and promoting a sense of calm.

Here's a breakdown of the 5S principles:

1. **Sort:** Keep only what you need and get rid of the rest. Declutter your belongings and identify the essentials that deserve a place in your home.

2. **Set in order:** Arrange items logically so they're easy to find and access. Frequently used items should be within easy reach, while less frequently used items can be stored further away.

3. **Shine:** Keep your storage areas clean and tidy. A clean and organised space is more inviting and makes it easier to maintain order.

4. **Standardise:** Create a consistent system for organising and labeling. This ensures that everyone in the household knows where things belong and how to put them away properly.

5. **Sustain:** Make it a habit to keep things organised. Regularly review and refine your storage systems to ensure they continue to meet your needs and promote a clutter-free environment.

By incorporating the 5S principles into your home design, you'll create a space where everything has its place, and everything is in its place. This not only saves time and reduces stress, but also fosters a sense of harmony and well-being. You'll never have to search for misplaced keys or wonder where that seldom-used kitchen gadget is stored. Everything will be in good working order and readily available when you need it.

Consider incorporating these smart storage ideas into your design:

- **Shallow shelves in pantries:** This makes it easy to see and access all your food items, preventing things from getting lost and expiring at the back.

- **Ample hanging space and drawers:** Design your wardrobes with a mix of hanging space and drawers to suit your clothing storage preferences.

- **Shallow drawers for small items:** This prevents items from disappearing into the depths of a drawer and makes it easier to find what you need.

- **Power points in bathroom drawers:** Keep hairdryers and other appliances neatly tucked away and ready to use.

- **Ledge shelves in showers:** Provide a designated spot for shampoos and cleansers, keeping your shower tidy and organised.

- **Pull-out rubbish bins:** Make it easy to dispose of kitchen scraps and keep your countertops clean.

A clutter-free home fosters a clutter-free mind, allowing you to focus on what truly matters.

CASE STUDY: Sally and Scott

Sally and Scott were living in Sydney but wanted to make a lifestyle change to Tasmania in their retirement years. They came to us with an interesting brief – they wanted a home that truly expressed their artistic personalities, something bold that made an impact on the street. The trouble was, they had quite different personalities. Sally is an extrovert who loves to cook and entertain, while Scott is a more reserved person who expresses himself through music.

The solution was to design two pavilions – the Light Side and the Dark Side. The Light Side featured a sun-filled space which used white cladding with a high ceiling and included an open-plan space through the kitchen and living and dining areas that flowed into a sunroom. The Dark Side was covered in black cladding and contained the more private areas of the home, including bedrooms, bathrooms and Scott's music studio. The two were linked by a glass walkway.

Scott's sound-proofed studio enables him to play music late into the night without disturbing Sally (or the neighbours). After his late-night sessions, Scott likes to sleep late, but Sally is an early riser. She likes to go straight to her professional-standard kitchen in the Light Side, which was designed to keep the appliance noise contained so Scott can sleep in. We designed a large walk-in pantry where she could store and use her equipment – Sally calls it her 'she shed'. It was custom-built to perfectly fit her tools and provides ample storage and working space which allows her to embrace her more complicated culinary projects while keeping the kitchen in the open-plan pavilion clear and clutter-free.

We built Sally and Scott's home in Tasmania while they were still in Sydney. We communicated daily and long before we began construction we had asked questions such as: 'What appliances do you own and what are their measurements?', 'Do you keep your flour in floor tubs or jars on the shelf?', 'How big is your drum kit?', 'Where will you place your amps and speakers and how will that affect the room's sound?', 'How much double hanging space do you need in your wardrobes for dresses and coats?' and 'How do you like to store your socks?' All of these questions may seem mundane or overly fastidious; however, it is the smaller details and the subtler nuances that make a house start to feel as though it is a home perfectly designed for *you*.

Livable housing

Livable housing means designing your floor plans to be accessible for everyone, to better accommodate people staying in their own home longer and ageing in a place they love, and to cater for people with higher mobility needs. Creating a floor plan that is livable is a big part of making sure your dream home is functional.

Australia has established the Livable Housing Design Guidelines,[8] which can certify a home to be either silver, gold or platinum level depending on the criteria it meets. Livable housing has generous space for circulation in all areas of a home, provisions for grab rails in showers and toilets, wider doorways, no steps to get in the house, a toilet on the ground floor if the home is more than one storey, kitchen and laundry facilities with wider dimensions between benches and walls, power points and light switches at certain heights, taps and door handles with levers rather than knobs, window heights low enough to make sure you can see outside, slip-resistant floor coverings and no steps between rooms or into showers.

Australia also has guidelines for specialist disability accommodation.[9]

Relationships

As you can see from Sally and Scott's story, an important aspect of designing a home layout is considering the impact of your activities on your loved ones, whether they be night owls or morning larks. Good design can contribute to harmonious relationships by ensuring each member of the household can complete their activities without negatively impacting others.

The effect of sound in your home is an important consideration – whether it's because you have a sleeping baby or you're a shift worker, whether you have a band rehearsing in the garage or power tools in use. You can soundproof areas or make spaces separate so that noisy activities don't disturb other members of the family. Consider other tension points that you might be able to head off with good design; for example, you can create a special play space for kids that contains the mess (but not the creativity) or add an extra bathroom.

Connection with the people who enter a home is another key aspect that can be included in the design. A living, socialising and cooking zone can encourage people to gather in the one area simply due to the design of the room, the joinery and the placement of the furniture. Your design has the power to automatically gather people together if that's what you desire.

DREAM HOME-WORK

Make a list of each room you would like in your home. Refer to the list in this chapter for help.

If you want to have a sketch before meeting your architect, as a first step in playing with home design on your particular site, map out the zones of your home. Start by making a rough sketch of your building site – use what you have learned in the last chapter and mark the direction of the best views, the pathway of the sun, the best access to the site, etc. Now experiment with optimising the zones of your home; for example, orient the living zone to catch the best view, and the rest and relax zone to be away from traffic noise. Once you have the zones situated in the best arrangement for your block, work on the arrangement of rooms within the zone.

Make a list of the habits you'd like to develop and the habits you'd like to change. Is there any way you can make your bad habits more difficult or inconvenient and your good habits easier through the design of your home?

Imagine making your favourite meal when thinking about your kitchen design. Go through the motions of locating each ingredient and utensil. Can you access everything easily and carry out the necessary tasks with the space you need, including disposing of waste and getting dishes out of the way? You can also do this with other working areas of your home, like the laundry or workshop.

Make a list of the things you struggle to store, such as suitcases, camping equipment, wetsuits or crystal glassware. What kind of storage would be ideal for these items? What items do you use on a regular basis and what do you only use once or twice a year?

FUNCTION

Make a list of precious items you want to keep or display in your home. Where will you put them? Are there any special requirements, eg temperature control for wine or protection from direct sunlight for works of art?

Are there areas of the home where pets might come and go and do they need a doggy door access and confined areas?

Overarching function statement

Can you list the rooms you want in your floor plan in the form of a few dot points that answer the question: 'What rooms do I need in my home?' It might be something like:

- 1 × entry with airlock and coat and shoe storage
- 1 × main bedroom with ensuite and walk-in wardrobe
- 2 × bedrooms with built-in wardrobes
- 1 × main bathroom
- 1 × separate powder room/toilet
- 1 × open-plan kitchen, living and dining area
- 1 × laundry
- Two-car enclosed garage
- 1 × deck

This will help you prioritise any competing considerations in your home design.

Write this statement on your Dream Home Journal.

Summary

The element of function looks at your home as a working space where activities need to be carried out in the most efficient way possible. A functional layout can minimise housework and clutter, solve storage issues and even support positive habits and reduce relationship tensions.

This element looks at different aspects to ensure your design meets these practical requirements. It also looks for efficiencies to suit your lifestyle and ways to take some of the tension out of daily life.

6
Feeling

If you are considering designing and building the home of your dreams, take a moment to imagine what that home would feel like. Notice that I asked what it would *feel* like rather than how it would look.

The feeling that comes from your home involves stirring all your senses – when you get the feeling right, you should feel positive and uplifted when you enter the space, and you should wake up refreshed, rejuvenated and inspired to live life and chase your goals. In essence, your home should make you feel happy.

In this chapter, we'll look at the way your home makes you feel, including its impact on your senses and your moods. This is the fun stuff where you bring in your design style, selections and the beautiful photos you've seen on Instagram and Pinterest. We'll look at how architects and interior designers work with your mood board and their own mood recipes to create an evocative feeling by combining the following ingredients: senses; moods; materials and texture; lighting; colour; fittings, fixtures and finishes; biophilic design; volume, space and scale.

The five senses

On a full immersion experience to an Airbnb as I lay on the window seat basking in the warmth of the sun and breathing in the fresh air, I couldn't help but be struck by the beauty of my surroundings – the timber-clad walls, the high ceiling, the shelves full of books from around the world. The aroma of the wood, warmed by the sun, filled my nostrils, and I felt a sense of inspiration and relaxation wash over me. It was in this moment of calm and refection that I realised the true impact our built environment has on our wellbeing. In this chapter, we will explore the five human senses and how they are affected by the spaces we inhabit.

The sense of smell

Smell has the power to transport you not only to a different place but also to a different time. Do you ever come across a smell that reminds you of something from your childhood, or perhaps a perfume that reminds you of someone who wears it? Planning the right amount of ventilation and the positioning of the garden and the sunlight can ensure your house smells sunny and fresh. What smell would you associate with your home?

The scent of your home will include what you do in it (baking bread, using essential-oil diffusers or perhaps displaying a vase of flowers) combined with the materials used in its construction, such as natural timbers. You can also create a scented garden to draw in the fragrance of, for example, lavender, citrus or eucalyptus. If you use materials like carpet with a high level of volatile organic compounds (VOCs), your rooms will smell like the release of airborne particulates or chemicals from the off-gassing.

The sense of touch

In terms of building your home, everything is tactile. You can (and will) touch each and every surface and material, from the walls to the flooring to the doors and windows. Think about what surfaces people will be touching in your home – for example, granite benchtops, concrete flooring, a wooden handrail or a brass tap.

The sense of hearing

This is the sense with which you pick up vibrations and detect activity. Your home has a voice of its own.

The sounds in the background of your living space are for you to choose. What three prominent sounds can you detect upon entering your home? For example, is it a fountain in the yard, music playing or wind chimes? Is it the noisy churning of the dishwasher, a heat pump/air conditioner or traffic noise?

Many people don't have clear ideas about where they want to place speakers around their home to listen to music or the radio or to connect with home entertainment systems. These elements are critical for creating a mood. Thinking about sound in your home also means thinking about how you would like to interact with natural sounds: the liberating joy of birdsong or the ancient swaying of wind in the trees. You might also like to have a water feature in your design or landscaping to create the tranquil sound of water running.

The sense of sight

One of the most inundated senses, because of technological advancement, is the sense of sight, yet you can create many effects with your visual space that can have a powerful effect on your mood.

The quality of light is a crucial factor when it comes to sight. Human eyes are not meant to be staring at computers under artificial light day in, day out. While it might not be possible for everyone to work away from the computer, it's possible to design your home in a way that allows the natural light to seep in and nourish not only your eyesight but also your other senses. Are there spots in your home which receive natural light? If not, can you identify areas that could have access to natural light and ventilation?

The sense of taste

The sense of taste is perhaps the most rewarding yet easy-to-activate sense, something fast-food manufacturers have been exploiting for decades. Flavour is so evocative that we use this sense as a metaphor to sum up the entirety of our personal style and aesthetic – our taste, by which we mean our collated aesthetic looks that express who we are. You might find it useful to think about what sort of flavour you would like to achieve in your home. Would you like to give visitors a sense of your home as sweet and fresh or rich and luxuriant? How would you define your style and taste? Does your current home capture it? What could be different?

> **EXERCISE: Emotion-Provoking Questions**
>
> Take some time to find a quiet and comfortable place where you can think without distractions. Now ask yourself these questions about your current home:
>
> - What's your favourite space in your current house?
> - Why do you love that space?

- What can you hear and smell in that space?
- What feeling does that space give you?
- What is the one-word emotion you associate with that space?
- Can you think of other individual emotion words?
- What do you need in your new home to get that feeling again?

By answering these questions, you can start to understand what is most important to you in your current home and what you want to achieve in your new home. It will help you communicate your needs and desires to your architect, making sure that your new home will be designed to meet your emotional needs as well as your practical ones.

Moods

Moods represent different emotional states and they are profoundly influenced by our senses. Take sound for example – many people turn on calming music when they feel like relaxing. Conversely, if you are trying to energise yourself, perhaps getting ready for a party, you are more likely to turn on upbeat music. Cinema sound designers have made a profession out of manipulating our emotional responses through carefully chosen sounds.

All of your senses have a powerful impact on your mood and, like a movie sound designer, you can mix carefully chosen sensual elements to create different moods in your home. You can choose to create a positive mood with the right mix but, of course, the wrong mix can create a negative mood. Here's a list of adjectives, good and bad, to describe the way your home could make you feel:

- Cheerful
- Reflective
- Gloomy
- Peaceful
- Focused
- Confined
- Humorous
- Idyllic
- Whimsical
- Romantic
- Calm
- Hopeful
- Angry
- Fearful
- Tense
- Lonely
- Playful
- Formal
- Creative
- Anxious
- Relaxing

Write down some sensual elements that you associate with each of these moods, both good and bad. For example, you may associate 'sunlight' with 'cheerful', 'eucalyptus' with 'focused' or 'machinery noise' with 'tense'. This list provides some suggestions for things you may want to enhance or minimise in different areas of your home.

Mood boards

Mood boards are collections (either online or physical collections like scrapbooks or shoeboxes) where you gather design elements that evoke a positive emotional response. Your mood boards should be combinations of sensual elements that evoke, for you personally, the mood you want to create.

Not everyone has the same emotional reaction to particular elements. For example, for some people, concrete benchtops offer a feeling of clean, modern order, while for others they seem cold and sterile.

Putting together a mood board is not just about picking things you like, it's also about picking things that evoke the moods you want in your home. Making this distinction will improve the value of your mood boards as briefing tools for your design team.

Mood recipes

Once you know the moods you want to create in different spaces of your home, and the kinds of sensual elements that evoke those moods for you and your family, you are ready to brief your design team on the look and feel of your home.

Your team, in turn, will combine these elements using what I call a 'mood recipe'. Just like a recipe for a dish, a mood recipe has ingredients that must be added in certain amounts and in a certain order and then cooked in a certain way. This is harder than it looks, which is why it's imperative to draw on professional advice.

A good design team will discuss the mood you'd like to create in different spaces in your home, and they'll use a mix of elements that draw on the five senses to create that mood using a recipe. For example, there's a recipe for creating calm, and a recipe for creating inspiration, and another for creating a playful mood.

Mood recipes usually include guidance around the selections (ingredients); in particular, whether they are natural or artificial, the amount of each selection used (quantities), and the installation (cooking). Let's take a look at some of the ingredients that a good design team keeps in the pantry.

Materials and texture

Different materials create different effects. Think of the difference between an exterior wall made of glass and an exterior wall made of plasterboard. A wall of glass creates a much more intimate relationship with the outside world, while white plasterboard is solid and clean. If it is used in the wrong way, some might find stark white plasterboard 'soulless'. There are places where plasterboard is the right choice to enhance a mood, but in other instances it will have the opposite effect – ultimately unravelling the mood you are trying to create.

The key aesthetic consideration for choosing materials is how natural you want your home to feel. Do you like the idea of a naturally weathered full-timber home, or does the idea of sharp lines and sleek surfaces appeal to you more?

CASE STUDY: Modern history

I recently completed a home for clients who were true collectors with a passion for preserving history. For over a decade they had been collecting stunning vintage pieces, including a century-old woodworking bench, antique sinks and reclaimed doors that showcase the craftsmanship of the past. They had considered renovating a heritage home but, having lived in one before, they knew how cold and draughty they could be. Instead, they commissioned a new home design to pay homage to the past while drawing on the best of modern sustainable building technology. During the build, we incorporated the couple's collected pieces, including salvaged timber doors in various shapes and sizes, reclaimed sinks and tapware. Custom-made light fittings, customised brass plumbing, and old-school tiles were also used to create a feeling of history in a brand-new home.

Closely related to materials is texture. This is both a visual and a tactile element and can have a strong effect on a room. You can introduce different textural elements into your design, such as smooth or rough surfaces, shiny or matt finishes and soft or hard furnishings. Texture plays a key role when you are selecting flooring, wall finishes, ceilings, benchtops, light switches and tiles.

Lighting

Lighting is the art of shaping atmosphere and emotion within your home, crafting a sensory experience that supports your well-being and enhances the beauty of your surroundings. It's about more than just visibility—it's about creating a symphony of illumination that dances throughout your home, day and night. During the day, invite the sun to be your primary light source. Carefully consider window placement and orientation to maximise natural daylight, allowing it to flood your spaces with warmth and energy. As evening descends, transition to a carefully orchestrated play of artificial light, layering different types and intensities to create a dynamic and inviting ambiance. Avoid the monotony of a single overhead fixture, opting instead for a thoughtful blend of ambient, task and accent lighting. Ambient lighting sets the foundation, providing overall illumination for general visibility and navigation. Task lighting, focused and functional, illuminates specific areas for activities like reading or cooking. Accent lighting adds the finishing touch, highlighting architectural features, artwork or creating a desired mood.

Embrace the power of high-quality light that mimics the natural qualities of sunlight, bringing vibrancy and depth to your living spaces. Colours will appear richer, textures will come alive, and the subtle details of your home will shine through. Artwork, furniture, even the food on your table, will be elevated by the interplay of light and shadow. Opt for high-quality LED fixtures with high Hertz drivers to ensure smooth, flicker-free illumination that's gentle on your eyes. Consider the activities performed in each room and choose fixtures that provide adequate lux levels (brightness) and appropriate beam angles for optimal comfort and function. The colour temperature of light subtly influences our mood and alertness. Embrace the natural cycle of daylight, opting for cooler tones during the day to promote focus and productivity, and warmer tones in the evening to encourage relaxation and prepare for sleep. Tunable lighting systems can mimic this natural progression, supporting your circadian rhythm and enhancing your overall well-being.

Embrace the convenience and energy efficiency of smart lighting systems. Program lights to turn on and off based on occupancy or time of day, and adjust brightness and colour temperature remotely to create the perfect ambiance for any occasion. Remember, the feeling of your home begins at the doorstep. Exterior lighting creates a welcoming first impression, enhances safety and security, and sets the stage for the experience within. Consider wall lights that accentuate the texture of your facade or subtle landscape lighting that casts a warm glow on your home. Explore the potential of recessed lighting, LED strips and other innovative solutions to create unique and personalised effects. Illuminate shower shelves, highlight architectural details or even add a touch of whimsy with under-stair lighting.

And finally, don't underestimate the timeless appeal of a fireplace. Its flickering light and warmth tap into a primal human connection, creating a sense of comfort and intimacy that technology alone can't replicate.

Colour

Colour sets the mood the moment you step into a home. Whether a historic house or a modern build, the colours you choose have a profound impact on the home's atmosphere. They can enhance the flow of natural light, instantly making a space feel welcoming or stark, and influence your emotions. Consider colour a powerful tool for transforming your house into your dream home. Below is a colour chart tool that outlines the emotions you can evoke with different colours.

Colour	Emotions
Red	Energises and grabs attention, perfect for creating bold statements or accenting key features
Orange	Injects warmth and social vibes, ideal for kitchens or entertaining spaces
Yellow	Uplifts the mood and sparks creativity, a great choice for work areas or playrooms
Green	Evokes feelings of peace and nature, ideal for bedrooms, bathrooms or relaxation areas
Blue	Promotes calmness and trust, perfect for living rooms or home offices
Purple	Hints at luxury and ignites imagination, a good choice for accent walls or creative spaces

Colour	Emotions
Pink	Creates a gentle and playful atmosphere, ideal for nurseries or guest rooms
Brown	Grounds a space and offers a sense of comfort, perfect for living rooms or libraries
Black	Adds sophistication and drama, use sparingly for a bold statement or to create depth
White	Opens up a space and feels clean, ideal for smaller rooms or creating a modern look
Grey	Provides a calming and neutral backdrop, allowing other design elements to shine
Beige	Creates a sense of warmth and tranquillity, great for a calming, neutral backdrop

Fittings, fixtures and finishes

You'll need to make dozens of decisions about these based on how they will work together. Fittings include appliances, plumbing fittings such as tapware, benchtops and joinery, light fittings, curtains and blinds, power points, bathroom accessories and door handles.

The choice seems endless. There are many materials, constructed in many different ways and with new technologies. The options keep increasing, while discontinued lines can leave some people short if they've misjudged their quantities. It's worthwhile working with an expert architect or interior designer who can help you navigate this area and bring the different selections together. They can communicate your selections clearly to the builder; for example, whether the tiles should be laid vertically or horizontally, in-line or off-centre, and what colour the grouting and silicone should be.

Keep in mind that these elements must work harmoniously with your decorating plans – your window dressing, artwork, wallpaper, plants and rugs.

Two types of detail

In the industry we talk about two types of detail – architects' details and builders' details. Architects' details are included in the specific plans they have spent months drawing up to ensure the building is constructed in exactly the way they imagined it. Builders' details relate to the way each part of the construction is put together. Every builder goes about their work in a slightly different way. Most architects' plans don't extend to this level of detail; however, the craftsmanship that goes into building your home is a crucial factor in how the end result feels. It's critical to have both an experienced architect and an experienced builder to achieve a quality dream home.

After finishing school in year ten, I struggled to find an apprenticeship, so I enrolled in a fine-furniture course with a desire to grow my skills. Looking back, this worked out perfectly. The course taught me things I didn't learn in my carpentry apprenticeship, such as how to read the grain of a piece of timber and how to sharpen tools to take precise millimetre shavings off a joint to make it fit perfectly. It showed me that I had a natural talent for working with wood and I quickly became the best student in my class with hand skills well beyond my years.

I came to understand the meaning of craftsmanship and the value of quality. I decided that whatever I did in life I would aim to achieve the same level of quality and precision. Quality work is about focusing on doing all the small things the best they can be done and cumulatively creating a project to a world class level. This core value of quality workmanship is, unfortunately, becoming rare in the building industry. It is, however, still a core value in my business. I take great pleasure from quality products and a well-finished home, and I am reputably asking my team, what does world class look like and are we continuously improving to achieve it.

To me, spending a bit more on the items you will be touching and using each day, like quality door handles, is important and can make or break a dream home.

Furniture

Ensure that any important pieces of your existing furniture, such as large beds, dining tables, pianos and any other special or large items, have a place where they will work well in the design. These should be measured and drawn into the floor plan to get a sense of the room and the space around it when they are in place.

Biophilic design

The concept of biophilic design is becoming more popular in the building industry. We have evolved in the modern world to a state where we are disconnecting ourselves from nature. Biophilic design aims to improve the connection between humans and the natural world through design features such as natural building materials, indoor plants, open windows, wide doors and access to the environment. Studies show connecting with nature helps with cognitive function, brain activity, blood pressure, mental health, immune function, heart rate variability and a reduction in cortisol, which is a stress hormone.

Environmental exposure can cause changes in epigenetic regulation. Studies have shown the link between environmental exposure and gene expression.[10,11,12] Being in nature alters the expression of thousands of our genes and our body starts working better. All building products come from nature, but not all are natural, so choose products that are natural and designed to connect with nature. Our built environment and natural environment should seamlessly connect. Have you ever gone away for a week or two on a camping trip or on holiday to a beach or mountain destination only to return home refreshed and rejuvenated? If so, do you think this is because you had time off work or because you spent less time in a toxic indoors environment and more time in nature?

In my home, I use lots of natural materials and lots of glass because I believe the closer we align to nature, the happier and healthier we become.

Volume, space and scale

The way a room in your home feels is about not only its size but also its volume and scale. A standard ceiling height of 2,400 millimetres may feel low and confining in a large room, while higher or raked ceilings can create a more open and airy feeling. Ceiling height affects the air volume, heating, cooling and acoustics of the room. The size and scale of materials used in the room can also impact its feel. Exposed ceiling rafters or beams that are too small or too big for the room's scale can create an uncomfortable atmosphere. The width of floorboards and their direction of installation can also affect the perception of the room's length and width. By carefully considering these factors, you can create a comfortable and functional living space.

DREAM HOME-WORK

If you've collected inspirational photos of dream home designs in a scrapbook or online, go through them and compare them to your home design. Make sure the elements that inspire you are included in your design.

Think about your favourite existing possessions, including your clothes. These pieces provide great insight into your style and can indicate the stable elements of your taste across the years. For example, do you like bold colours or neutral tones? Do you prefer minimalist lines or are you a fan of classic or heritage design? Make sure your home design reflects your taste and style.

Think about the materials, fittings and fixtures in your home design. Do these align with your taste? For example, do you like sleek modern surfaces or do you prefer the look of weathered timbers with a story to tell?

Think through how you will furnish and decorate your home, including paint colours, the placement of important pieces of furniture, window and bed dressings, pot plants, rugs and other details. Consider how these will interact with your home design. Also consider how your home design will adapt to changes in fashion and taste in years to come.

What is your top priority for the interior design of your home? Do you have a specific tile, bench top material, colour or finish that you love? Do you require ample storage space? Challenge yourself to choose things you are passionate about.

Is there anything you strongly dislike when it comes to interior design? Is there a particular style or colour you cannot stand?

What colours and textures would you like to be surrounded by in your home?

Do you have any favourite brands of appliances, tapware or other household items that you are passionate about?

Are there any appliances or furnishings you would like to bring into your new home? If you have recently purchased a fridge or other appliance, let your team know so that it can be planned into the design of your new kitchen. Similarly, if you have furnishings you would like to incorporate, your team can work to create a colour palette or style that complements them.

Overarching feeling statement

Can you envisage living in your new home environment? Can you list the feeling you want to create in a few dot points? For example, 'I want my home to feel calm and fresh' or 'I want my home to feel rustic and natural'.

Write this down in your Dream Home Journal.

Summary

The feeling in your home is created by layering many details that appeal on a sensual level. It's possible to create a range of moods using mood recipes, combining details that evoke different moods for you personally, and it's important to work with a professional team who can help you to identify and create the environments you want in your home. In this chapter we've looked at the way different elements of design can be used to create moods in your home.

7
Health

A good home design can support your health, while a bad one might be actively making you sick. Many people get caught up in the colours, textures and materials without considering the impact their home has on their health. In this chapter, we'll examine SBS, which we touched on in Chapter 1, and look at ways to avoid creating environmental sickness in your home and the implications of using toxic materials. We'll also look at decisions that support your physical and emotional wellbeing in the areas of water, air/ventilation, temperature, light (natural and artificial) and electromagnetic fields.

When buildings make us sick

The enormous impact our built environment has on our health is often overlooked. We wouldn't actively decide to construct a building that makes us sick, but sometimes this is what ends up happening. Before we delve further into the ways our home impacts our health, let's cover some key terminology.

Building biology

There are people who specialise in the health of a building, called building biologists. Building biology originated in Germany in the 1960s.[13] It emerged as a response to increasing concerns about the adverse effects of modern building practices on human health and the environment. The concept of building biology is a holistic approach that examines the intricate connection between the built environment, human health and the surrounding ecosystem. Building biology emphasises the importance of using natural and non-toxic building materials to optimise indoor air quality, and considers the relationship between the built environment and the surrounding ecosystem. The main goal is to achieve harmony among these three elements, creating living spaces that support wellbeing and sustainability. By rating building materials for their compatibility with environmental factors, building biologists aim to create spaces that promote physical wellbeing, mental health and environmental sustainability.

Sick building syndrome

SBS is a term used to describe health problems linked to buildings. According to the Australian Government Department of Climate Change, Energy, the Environment and Water, SBS can describe symptoms such as irritation in the skin, eyes or throat, headaches, drowsiness, fatigue, difficulty concentrating and irritability. In the long term, exposure to chemicals (such as formaldehyde) and microscopic fibres (such as asbestos) can even cause cancer or respiratory disease.[14,15]

Let's look at some of the factors that can lead to unhealthy homes, all of which are key considerations for building biologists when they determine building ratings.

Water

It is essential to prioritise the quality of the water we drink and use in our daily lives, and consider how water plays a role in the way we structure our homes.

Dehydration is the leading cause of daytime fatigue, nausea, constipation and headaches. Even a small drop in hydration can result in a significant loss of energy. A lack of hydration doesn't affect just what's inside our bodies, it also affects our skin, especially when combined with contaminants such as chlorine. That's where a water filtration system comes in.

It is not just drinking unfiltered water that can impact on healthy functioning, it is also about showering, bathing and cooking with contaminant-free water. Studies suggest that chlorine absorption from a ten-minute shower is equivalent to drinking eight glasses of unfiltered tap water, as the chlorine can enter your body through your skin.[16] Water filtration can improve the taste of water, soften hair, create healthier skin and reduce the need for heavy-duty chemicals when cleaning. Additionally, filtered water can protect appliances from calcium damage, increasing energy efficiency in water heating appliances and reducing the need for plastic-bottled water, thus reducing our environmental impact. Some filters remove contaminants down to 1 micron in size and eliminate limescale throughout the entire home without wasting water or adding to your water bill.

There are solutions of water filtration that not only filter out harmful chemicals but also preserve healthy minerals in the water. These include the following systems:

- **A reverse osmosis (RO) water filter** uses a semipermeable membrane to remove impurities from water. It also has stages of sediment filtration, activated carbon block filtration and remineralisation to add healthy minerals back into the water. Installing an RO water filter in a new home can provide the freshest, purest and healthiest drinking water possible.

- **Ultraviolet-C (UVC) treatment water filter systems** are a type of system that physically disinfects water by using ultraviolet light to inactivate microorganisms. They work by exposing water to ultraviolet light, which disrupts the DNA of microorganisms such as bacteria, viruses and cysts. This process makes the microorganisms unable to reproduce, effectively disabling these biological contaminants in the water. These systems can be used for treating rainwater, bore water and other sources of water that may contain harmful bacteria or viruses. One of the benefits of UVC treatment systems is that they do not require any chemicals to disinfect the water. This means that the water is not altered in any way and there is no risk of chemical residue or by-products. UVC treatment systems are also easy to install and maintain, requiring only periodic lamp replacement to ensure effective treatment.

If you are harvesting rainwater on-site, it's worth considering the material you choose for your water tanks. For example, polyvinyl chloride (PVC) contains bisphenol A (BPA), which has been found to be an endocrine disruptor linked to cancer and heart disease.[17] Pipes and tanks with PVC bladders can leach PVC into the water. Generally, water supplied to homes must be stored in food-grade tanks, so it's worth ensuring all your tanks meet this requirement, especially if you plan to water food plants, such as a veggie garden, with stored rainwater.

Perfluoroalkyl and polyfluoroalkyl substances (PFAS) are a group of artificial chemicals that resist heat, water and oil, earning them the nickname 'Forever Chemicals'. They do not break down easily in the environment and can travel long distances through waterways. These chemicals were created in the 1950s and are found in various products – for example, non-stick pans. PFAS have been linked to adverse health effects, such as cancer, thyroid hormone disruption and immune system dysfunction. Studies have found that water throughout the world is contaminated with PFAS.

Moisture, condensation and mould

Water vapour is created by many everyday activities like breathing, cooking, drying clothes, showering, boiling the kettle and keeping indoor plants, and it can be released from building materials when buildings are heated. The rate of water vapour accumulated in your home depends on your individual circumstances, but a typical home can generate up to 20 litres of water vapour every day.

Many older homes are poorly insulated and draughty (meaning they leak air). In recent years there has been a push towards constructing buildings which use less energy (ie they have higher star rating for energy). This means more insulation and buildings that are better sealed against air leakage. Theoretically, this reduces energy consumption and the costs associated with heating and cooling – which is a positive for keeping warm, maintaining energy efficiency and reducing carbon emissions. In a well-insulated and airtight home, however, heat and moisture retention can become a problem. Without the opportunity to escape the building envelope, moisture in the building can build up and air quality decreases (more on that later).

If there is sufficient water vapour in the air, it will condense when it comes into contact with a cold surface. More water vapour and colder surfaces mean more condensation.

Condensation can be thought of as the opposite of evaporation, and the conditions which cause condensation are the opposite of the conditions which cause evaporation, as shown in the table below.

The best conditions for evaporation	The opposites of the factors that cause evaporation, which lead to condensation
High surface temperature	Low surface temperature
Low ambient humidity	High ambient humidity
Air movement	Still air
Exposed to sunlight and heat	Sheltered and shaded
Vapour permeable materials	Vapour impermeable materials

What is the problem with all this moisture build-up? Mould. Mould can grow whenever the air exceeds 70% relative humidity and above. Homes must be consistently below 70% relative humidity to be free of problematic mould. Research shows that if the temperature drops below 18 degrees Celsius in a house, most people turn on their heating. In a place like Launceston, Tasmania, it's below 18 degrees Celsius about 80% of the time. Once the heating is switched on, the inside temperature is different from the outside, which creates the risk of condensation and mould. You can buy an inexpensive humidity sensor for your home to monitor this.

Condensation and mould are worryingly common issues in Australian homes, even in newly constructed buildings. Studies by organisations like CSIRO and AIBS highlight the prevalence of these problems. Dr Mark Dewsbury from the University of Tasmania conducted a study of condensation in residential buildings in 2016.[18] He found that Australia has twice the asthma rate of other developed countries and is the only developed country that does not have guidelines around condensation and mould in buildings. He estimates this costs the country AU$10 billion per year, from medical costs to chronic disease treatment.

Unfortunately, condensation can't be stopped – it is an inevitable side effect of energy efficiency because we are creating a bigger temperature difference between the inside and the outside of our homes, and minimising airflow through the building. The risk of condensation will generally increase at higher energy ratings and greater air tightness. The good news is, condensation can be managed effectively by good design and construction.

An ideal home design should allow moisture to be managed, maintaining overall air quality. Think of the outer skin of your building as a raincoat. When I was growing up on the farm, we had plastic raincoats. When I was working hard, my raincoat would keep in both the warm air *and* the water vapour (sweat). It wasn't until years later when I had my first Gore-Tex coat that I felt comfortable. My coat would keep out the rain and wind, keep in the warm air and let out the water vapour. This is the principle behind modern building membranes. Managing moisture levels inside the building assembly is the goal, which we'll look at closely in Chapter 8.

Air

After the 2019 bushfires in Australia, people have become more aware of the health implications associated with air quality. Contaminated air isn't always as easy to detect as smelling the effects of wood fires. Sometimes the contaminants are so microscopic they are not immediately detectable to humans. Particle pollution from fine particulates in the air not only irritates and causes inflammation of sensitive airways, those particulates can also cross semipermeable membranes in lung tissues into the blood. It is important to be informed about the quality of the air we breathe and how it impacts on our health.

Air quality

Air pollution, including high particulate air matter, has been associated with many chronic health problems and in 2016 was associated with 6.1 million deaths globally. The Commonwealth Scientific and Industrial Research Organisation has estimated that poor indoor air quality may be costing Australia as much as AU$12 billion per year due to sickness and resulting loss of productivity.[19]

Carbon monoxide

Carbon monoxide, a deadly gas that is impossible to see, taste or smell, can build up in any home with gas appliances, poorly installed fireplaces or wood-burning stoves. It can cause fatigue, chest pain, angina, impaired vision, dizziness, headaches, confusion, nausea, flu-like symptoms and even death. Gas stoves, heaters, wood stoves and fireplaces must be vented to the outside and all appliances must be installed properly to avoid leaking carbon monoxide. Fireplaces must have an operational flue damper and chimneys must be properly sealed.[20] If you are going to use gas appliances in your home, it is strongly recommended to install a carbon monoxide sensor to monitor levels.

Dust and dander

Health issues can also be caused by a build-up of dust, pet dander and hair, any of which can trigger allergies and asthma. These can be reduced by designing homes that are easy to keep clean or have a mechanical ventilation system.

Volatile organic compounds and spores

Certain substances – including paint, varnish, resins, glues, carpets, cleaners, disinfectants, degreasers, thinners, solvents, fuels, aerosol sprays, pesticides and other chemicals – release dangerous gases over time into the air, even when they're stored properly. This slow emission of gases is often referred to as 'off-gassing'. This happens because many of these products often contain VOCs such as formaldehyde and xylene or semi-volatile organic compounds (SVOCs) – a group of compounds that vapourise less readily than VOCs. Both groups have been linked to a myriad of health complications, including cancer development.[21] While VOCs can easily vapourise and release into the air (off-gas), SVOCs tend to be more persistent and can accumulate over time in indoor environments. Common household products contain these substances.

One design tip is to include at least one lockable cupboard in your laundry or garage to store these types of substances and prevent children from accessing them. In our home, we use only natural cleaning products, as it's better for both our family and the waterways after they go down the sink.

As discussed above, mould from built-up condensation can release spores into the home, resulting in allergic reactions, respiratory problems and asthma.[22]

CASE STUDY: Sydney mould

When I was growing up, I unknowingly lived in mouldy houses. Now I can sense a mouldy room as soon as I enter it. On a trip to Sydney, I checked in to my room and as soon as I arrived, I noticed the smell of mould. I was planning to only sleep there, as I had full days of meetings, but after two hours I had a headache and felt almost like I had a hangover.

I decided to pack up my things and move to new accommodation because I knew the harm a mouldy environment could have on my health. Even though my meeting was the next day, I still felt foggy, and it wasn't until the following day I started to feel like myself again. This was a strong reminder that mould toxins are awful for cognitive performance and our health and wellbeing. Low levels of mould make me less productive and high levels over the long term have known health effects I want to stay clear of.

Temperature

Both high and low indoor temperatures have been associated with health complications. According to the World Health Organization, unstable temperatures can harm the cardiovascular and immune systems, and heatwaves (which are increasing due to climate change) are linked with more deaths in the home.[23] Cold indoor temperatures can have even worse effects, including an increased risk of respiratory conditions, an increased risk of cardiovascular and circulation issues, and death.[24] The recommended healthy temperature range for homes is 18 degrees Celsius to 23 degrees Celsius. Heatwaves are going to become one of the major health factors that cause illness and death as the climate changes. Homes with PV solar panels and built to the Passivhaus Standard can use the heatwave to cool the house within an hour if the buildings are designed using the appropriate technology.

Light

A bright and well-lit space can boost your creativity, while a dingy corridor with no lighting can dampen your mood. In my home, I have ensured there is a part of the home with direct sunlight where I can sit. Warm sunlight increases your serotonin levels, lifts your mood and boosts your mitochondria function. It's important to spend time in natural light, rather than in the 'junk light' provided by LEDs and compact fluorescent lights. The UK government's Health and Safety Executive has highlighted the health impact of bright and flickering lights, which can cause irritation and fatigue. It recommends using natural lighting where possible, avoiding glare, flicker and noise and putting in controls to adjust levels of light.[25]

Natural light can be incorporated into designs via windows, glass doors or skylights. The clever use of eaves can also manage the light flow into your home. In summer, long eaves can block the sun when it is high in the sky. In winter, when the sun is lower in the sky, it can shine under the low eaves into your home.

An important consideration is the type of glass you choose, as different types can let different levels of UV into the building. Normal glass absorbs 97% of sunburn-causing UVB and 37% of UVA.[26] The recommended UV exposure depends on your geography. For example, you may want to minimise the UV in northern Australia and maximise the UV in the southern states. Any glass will reduce the levels of the sun's heat coming into the home – this is called the solar heat gain coefficient. Even a 4 millimetre clear glass panel will absorb about 25% of the sun's heat as it passes through. Thicker glass and more layers of glass (eg double glazing) increase this effect. Some glass treatments (like low-E glass) and tints will further decrease the entry of heat through the panels, which can be useful in hot climates.

Electromagnetic fields

Electromagnetic fields (EMFs) have become a prevalent aspect of modern life, stemming from power lines, mobile phones, Wi-Fi, 5G, Bluetooth, electric appliances, meter boxes, wiring, solar panels and inverters. There are six styles of frequencies on the electromagnetic radiation spectrum:

1. AC electrical fields
2. DC electrical fields
3. AC magnetic fields
4. DC magnetic fields
5. Microsurge electrical pollution (dirty electricity)
6. Radio-frequency radiation

Scientific debate surrounds the potential harm of EMFs on human health, with some studies raising concerns about their negative impacts. These include possible links between Wi-Fi and cellular DNA damage, neuropsychiatric effects, sperm/testicular damage, endocrine changes and calcium overload.[27] As more people seek to reduce EMF exposure, especially in sleeping areas, designing homes to mitigate the impact becomes crucial.

Wellbeing

We have talked about everything that can go wrong, but what are the considerations we can make in our builds for ultimate wellbeing?

Dedicated spaces to relax and recharge, for example through meditation, reading in the sun or taking a bath, are vital for mental health and wellbeing. Managed exposure to the built environment has also been shown to create positive emotions, strengthen resilience and lower the health impacts of stress, and it has been linked to reduced anxiety and depression.[28,29] You can design your home to maximise your connection with nature by using natural materials such as timber and stone. You can also create easy transitions between inside and outside, and use plants and natural elements around your home.

CASE STUDY: Health in my home design

I have had recurrent health issues for most of my adult life. After a trip to Thailand in 2009, I came home with a stomach parasite that took several years to diagnose and treat. I haven't been chronically ill, but since then I have often been in a less-than-optimal state, struggling with energy, contracting glandular fever and having a weakened immune system that left me vulnerable to frequent infections.

A defining moment came after my two kids were born and I struggled to find the energy and strength in my back to play with them after a day's work. I was even struggling with finding the energy to do my job. That point in my life taught me that my health is everything: if I don't have my health, I can't do anything else.

I began to look at how my home and office were affecting my health and wellbeing – the impacts of toxic materials and mould and how they could also be harming my family – and I looked into the ways home design could improve my health.

Here are some of the design hacks I've used to build health and wellbeing into our new home design:

- **Water:** We have purpose-built water filters, one on the outside of the house before the water comes in, and special water filters in the kitchen for drinking water only.
- **Air:** To keep it nice and warm, our home is fully sealed and insulated and it uses Passivhaus Standard, lowering the chances for mould to form. We'll also use a mechanical ventilation with heat recovery system (MVHR), which will suck out the stale air and bring in fresh air from outside while minimising heat loss.
- **Light:** We've included full blackout blinds in the bedrooms so we can sleep in complete darkness. They are automated to open with the sunrise, to support our natural circadian rhythm. We have also installed amber light for use in the evening, which is a different light spectrum to damaging blue light and will support our sleep patterns. For example, in the ensuite bathroom, we have amber lighting underneath the cupboards at floor level, which provides just enough light to use the bathroom at

night but not enough light to make our bodies think the sun is coming up.

- **Natural world:** We have floor-to-ceiling glass in our main living area, to let the sunlight flood into our home and connect us with the natural world. The entire building is built with timber for a natural feel, and we've brought nature right into our home by designing shelving specifically for indoor plants.
- **Wellbeing:** We have a yoga and ju-jitsu training area so we can easily roll out our mats, and there's storage for our weights, resistance bands, foam rollers and other equipment. We have also designed an outdoor bathtub, a sauna and a cold-plunge pool where we can rest and recuperate.

Health is a huge priority area for me, and my home is designed to support my health and wellbeing, and that of my family, on every level.

Sleep

Sleep is one of the most important things you will do in your home, yet it is often overlooked in home design. According to the Harvard Medical School, poor sleep can affect your judgement, mood and ability to learn and retain information. It can also increase your risk of serious accidents and injury. Long term it can lead to obesity, diabetes and heart disease.[30] Lack of sleep can also lower your life expectancy – people who sleep five hours or less per night have a 15% greater risk of dying from any cause.[31] Around one-third of Australians experience insomnia at some point in their lives.[32]

The most common cause of insomnia is poor sleep habits, which are otherwise known as 'sleep hygiene'. Bedrooms should be designed for optimal sleep – including attention to temperature (ideally around 18 degrees Celsius), air quality, light, EMFs and noise. For adults, bedrooms should be designed for two activities.[33]

Studies have found that light can disrupt our circadian rhythm, which regulates our body clock, and the blue light emitted by electronic devices is the most disruptive at night.[34] Your home design should encourage electronic equipment to be stored and charged outside the bedroom. Light sources should have low-light options in the amber spectrum where possible.

If we connected all the hours we spend sleeping into one consecutive sleep, most people would sleep for about twenty-eight years straight (based on sleeping eight hours per day and living to eighty-four years old). It's absurd that architects and designers put hardly any focus on designing bedrooms for optimum sleep. One of my favourite smartphone apps is linked to a ring I wear on my finger with built-in sensors that track my sleep cycle, which means I don't have to have my phone in my bedroom to track my sleep. Once I started to track and measure my REM, deep and light sleep, I could then test different things to improve it.

Traditional light bulbs can inhibit sleep quality by shutting off your natural melatonin production, whereas amber or red lights let your body respond as though it were dark. If you need to get up in the night, amber or red lighting will help you to fall back to sleep more easily. We have a light switch for normal light and a switch for amber lights in our bathrooms. I find that my kids naturally go for the amber light at bedtime or if they wake up through the night.

Exercise

However you like to keep fit, your home should cater for the physical activities you love. That might include room to practise yoga, lift weights or practise martial arts, or room to store the fitness equipment you use elsewhere (such as bikes, skis or kayaks). As we saw in Chapter 5, you can support your own fitness habits by making it easy to exercise.

Sauna

One of the best built environments humans have developed for health is the sauna, and the infrared sauna in particular. Saunas can penetrate deep into your skin, creating a cardiovascular workout while removing heavy metals and toxins via sweat. They reduce pain, help you lose weight, improve sleep and help with fitness and recovery. A sauna is a great addition to your dream home for boosting health, and a great place to relax.

DREAM HOME-WORK

Think about sleeping in the bedrooms of your home, especially noticing things like noise levels at night, light, air quality, temperature extremes in summer and winter, and any EMFs. Does your home design provide everything needed to support restful sleep?

Think about the air quality in your home. Can all rooms be ventilated?

Are you going to have a mould problem? Are bathrooms vented outside?

Are you using impermeable or permeable building materials?

Will you invest in better windows?

Consider the ways in which light enters your home and how this might change over the course of the day – is there enough natural light during the day and can you cut out harmful blue light at night?

Now you know what VOCs are, ask about the materials being used in your home. Will you make different material choices?

Consider asking manufacturers of 'low VOC' or 'zero VOC' products whether their products contain any SVOCs, such as: antimicrobials, pesticides, flame retardants, BPA, phthalates, PFAS, stain repellents and preservatives.

Overarching health statement

What is your key health priority for your home? Can you distil it down to a few dot points, such as: 'I want natural light to flood into my home', 'I want excellent ventilation to avoid mould' or 'I want low-toxic building materials used throughout'. This will help your design team determine your priorities.

Write this down in your Dream Home Journal.

Summary

Health and wellbeing are crucial aspects of home design that are often overlooked. A good home design can actively support your health, while a bad one can make you sick.

In this chapter we've looked at SBS and the ways your home has the potential to harm you, as well as the many design elements you can use to strengthen your health.

8
Technology

When we think of technology, it's easy to fall prey to imagining computers, electronics and phones, but technological advances mean so much more than just new gadgets. Oxford Dictionary defines technology as 'the application of scientific knowledge for practical purposes, especially in industry'. Across the construction industry, there have been exciting advances in the way buildings are designed. Factors such as the durability and longevity of materials, the optimisation of building techniques and the implementation of artificial intelligence, automation, digitalisation and data analysis have all meant we have more control over our built environments. Suffice it to say, advances in design technology and techniques are improving our ability to respond to the demands of the changing climate.

Using the latest techniques can help you build a unique, comfortable and healthy home, a home that is energy-efficient, structurally sound and cheaper to run. Building to a high standard and using materials that have longevity is sustainable – build a house that lasts longer and you build fewer houses overall, saving energy and resources.

Unfortunately, to apply the latest technology and build an advanced home, you'll have to look beyond the current building codes and practices. The construction industry as a whole has been slow to adopt new technologies and methods. Australia's NCC is the *minimum* requirement for building in Australia and stipulates a basic minimum level of health and comfort in homes. It does not specifically require that built houses provide the opportunity for optimum health and comfort for the occupants. Some green building practices like passive solar design and net zero principles focus only on energy consumption, not human comfort.

Market failure is often a precipitating factor driving government regulation. If the market doesn't self-correct then the government has to step in and create regulation. That's why it is important for homeowners to understand the basics of building standards and building science – so they can ask their architect and builder informed questions and drive change in the industry.

In this chapter we'll look at the new technological advancements you can consider to improve the sustainability, convenience, health and comfort of your home. We will explore building standards and the NCC; the building envelope; certified Passivhaus Standard, including heat and maintaining optimal thermic conditions; energy use and energy-saving techniques; and smart homes.

If you find any of the information too complex, you can always ask your architect or builder to read this chapter and implement some of the technical content.

Building standards and the National Construction Code

There are a number of different performance requirements (not to be confused with Australian Standards) for building your new home. Let's take a look through them, from the basic legal provisions to the premium standard of building construction.

The NCC is the minimum legal standard for construction in Australia. It is Australia's primary set of technical design and construction provisions for buildings, and sets the minimum required level for the safety, health, amenity, accessibility and sustainability of certain buildings. It includes detailed provisions but also references dozens of Australian Standards to provide clarity on construction and compliance across a range of facets, including restrictions on building in bushfire-prone areas, inclusions for disability access, timber-framing requirements, wet area waterproofing and so on.

Unlike building physics, the NCC is subject to human politics. Paradoxically, a brand-new building could comply with the latest NCC guidelines and still have significant potential for mould and discomfort.

Recently I saw a home where the owners had tried to do the right thing by building a highly insulated home to improve energy efficiency. The designer, building surveyor and builder all did the right thing according to the NCC, but the building physics had been overlooked and moisture had built up to such a degree that mould had infested the wooden frame of the house. This affected the structural integrity of the house and made it unsafe for human occupation. Once the problem reached this level, the house had to be partly demolished. This is obviously an expensive and time-consuming job – and it left the family without a home for months. A preoccupation with purely energy-efficient homes can lead to consequential outcomes.

The good news is, it's possible to design homes that are properly insulated and tightly sealed for maximum energy efficiency while still allowing moisture to be managed. Unfortunately, the NCC has not yet incorporated these design strategies as requirements, and thus the standards in the building industry have not caught up. If you don't know about, and ask for, high-quality solutions, builders will use the cheapest solutions that meet NCC standards. They might use wall membranes that are not vapour permeable, they may cut corners when installing insulation, leaving gaps where mould can form, or they may not fully waterproof a bathroom. No one should be building to the minimum building code – it's set as a minimum but it is not the smartest way to build a house.

Though my recommendation is to build to Passivhaus Standard if possible for your project, as I will discuss below.

The building envelope

Building science is the study of how air, moisture and heat move through a building's outer layer, which is called the building envelope. By understanding these movements, we can improve the performance and durability of our homes and buildings and avoid costly problems that can arise from poor building practices.

There are some important principles of building science to keep in mind when designing and building a home. One principle is that hot air rises and cool air sinks, so it's important to consider ventilation and insulation. Another principle is that air moves from hot to cold, so proper insulation is essential to keep heat inside during colder months and outside during warmer months. Water moves from wet to dry, which means that a good drainage system is important to keep water from entering and damaging the building. Finally, air and gas move from high pressure to low pressure, so it's important to consider airtightness and ventilation when designing a home to prevent drafts and maintain indoor air quality.

The primary reason we construct buildings with floors, walls and roofs is to create a safe and comfortable space we can control, despite external conditions. With changing climate conditions, however, buildings must be constructed to withstand harsh weather conditions such as heat, floods and storms. To ensure energy efficiency and durability, it is essential to prioritise the quality of the building envelope when designing your building, taking a 'fabric first' approach. This involves focusing on getting the building fabric right, rather than relying on active heating, air conditioning, solar panels and other additions to compensate for a poorly constructed building envelope. Experts recommend using WUFI (Wärme Und Feuchte Instationär), a software program that can simulate how heat and moisture move through a building's envelope.[35] By using WUFI, architects, builders and homeowners can get a better understanding of how their home will perform in different weather conditions, which can help them make informed decisions about insulation, ventilation and other design elements.

TECHNOLOGY

There are four main building control layers that make up the building envelope. These are (in order of importance to the build) the water control layer, the air control layer and the thermal and vapour control layer. Each layer serves a different function. For example, the water control layer ensures that occupants are kept dry, while the air control layer is designed to prevent air leakage that impacts on building durability and thermal control.

Water control: external wall and roof materials

A critical component of any building is a robust water control layer. This layer acts as a shield, preventing water intrusion and protecting the building's structure and interior from external moisture damage. Think of it as a water resistive membrane that envelops your home, ensuring that rain and wind are kept at bay.

Both your wall cladding and roofing play a role in this water resistive layer. Wall cladding acts as a rainscreen, deflecting the majority of rain and preventing it from reaching the underlying structure. However, some water may still penetrate this outer layer, making the water control layer essential. This layer, typically a water resistive membrane or sheathing, is installed beneath the cladding, providing a secondary line of defence against water and wind.

Similarly, your roof cladding sheds water away from the building, but a reliable water control layer beneath the roofing material ensures that any leaks or breaches are contained, preventing damage to the roof structure and the interior of your home.

Choosing the right materials for your external walls is crucial to achieving the desired look and functionality of your home. There are various options available, including metal, timber, hempcrete, rammed earth, brick, straw, concrete, cement sheets, lightweight concrete, aluminium, stone and tile, each with their own unique benefits and characteristics, and influence on the home's appearance, durability and environmental impact.

Air and vapour control: air tightness and air quality

An airtight building prevents convection (the flow of air through the building assembly) between the inside of the building and the outside. The main goal of airtightness is to maintain the durability of the building structure. An airtight barrier also prevents moisture from escaping when the temperature inside is different from the temperature outside, which means it should be designed carefully.

Buildings should have adequate air and moisture flow, as both these factors affect how healthy and comfortable the building is to live in. Optimal airtightness prevents draughts and temperature differences, is more energy-efficient and ensures more acoustically comfortable rooms. Think of it like a puffer jacket.

TECHNOLOGY

A puffer jacket is warmer than a jumper because it's stuffed full of feathers (insulation), but if you put on your big puffy jacket and don't zip it up, you'll still get cold. That's because it's not airtight. The first thing you need to do is zip it up to keep in the warmth and save energy usage. Now, if you had a hole in your jacket and you were to mend it with clear plastic, it wouldn't be as effective. You'd start to lose heat. It's the same with windows – they aren't as good at keeping in the heat. Even a high-quality, triple-glazed window still performs worse than a standard insulated wall. Of course, you don't want to remove all your windows, because as humans we need to have that indoor–outdoor connection. Like everything else with building, you need to weigh up your options.

Building an airtight home and using filtered air also means you have greater control over your indoor air quality even when there are outdoor air pollutants such as bushfire smoke or dust. Apps tracking air quality and air pollution such as **https://aqicn.org/map/australia** have become popular in Australia in recent years, especially after the devastating bushfires of 2019–20.[36] The level of carbon dioxide concentration in a house is a crucial factor in ensuring good indoor air quality. In Australia, it is essential to consider the air change ratio when designing an energy-efficient home and to engage a blower door test to make sure you are not going to be at risk of having high carbon dioxide levels. Ideally, the combination of an airtight building envelope with a good-quality filter on the house ventilation system can work to improve the air quality of the building.

The level of carbon dioxide concentration in a house is a crucial factor in ensuring good indoor air quality. The safe level of carbon dioxide concentration in a home is typically around 400–1,000 parts per million. If it exceeds this level, it can cause a range of health issues such as headaches, dizziness and increased heart rate. A standard-sized bedroom with no ventilation and two people sleeping in it can reach 1,000 parts per million within an hour.

In Australia, it is essential to consider the air change ratio when designing an energy-efficient home and get a blower door test to make sure you are not going to be at risk of having high carbon dioxide levels. The range of ratios are n50 tested air change ratio @ 50Pa pressure difference.

- n50: < 0.6ACH: Passivhaus certified
- n50: < 3: mechanical ventilation is mandatory
- n50: < 5: moisture becomes an issue
- n50: < 10: most average Class 1 homes in Australia will sit around here

Better building membranes, plus improved glazing, plus improved insulation are likely to equal the need for mechanical ventilation.

Mechanical ventilation with heat recovery (MVHR)

There is a simple way to let fresh air into your home without having to open your windows and let out the warm inside air. The system is called mechanical ventilation with heat recovery. Ideally, a home should be highly airtight with controlled ventilation. As the saying goes, 'build tight, ventilate right'. In warm climates, opening windows is the simplest method of controlled ventilation provided someone is home and the outside temperature is suitable. In cold climates, it is not practical to open windows for much of the winter and still maintain the home's warmth. In these cases, especially if the house is built to a high air tightness level, an MVHR is strongly recommended. It encompasses a fan and manifold that swaps the polluted and heated internal air with fresh outside air. The bonus of an MVHR is managing the levels of carbon dioxide, moisture, VOCs, dust, pollen and energy use in a building.

The warmer the air is in a house, the more water vapour that air can carry. Warm air is like a sponge, able to absorb lots of water, and when it's cold outside, most of us want our internal air temperature to be warm. The aim of a good build is to maintain the moisture in the air to an acceptable level. There are two main ways to manage vapour: remove the moisture from the air and let the moist air escape from the building.

Walls and ceilings rely on diffusion through a vapour-permeable material to transport the water vapour from the air. Mass transfer (allowing air to escape) is 100 times more effective at removing moisture in the air than diffusion. Up to 10 litres of hot air per minute can escape from a room out of a downlight hole into the ceiling. You can allow air to leak from a building to remove the water vapour effectively, but you will also lose the heat, and therefore this is not good for energy efficiency.

Thermal control

Unfortunately, Australians have accepted poor-quality housing as the norm. We often think of Australia as a hot continent, but in reality the majority of Australians live in areas where more energy is needed to keep them warm than is needed to keep them cool. In fact, we have a 20–30% greater death rate in winter than summer, which is higher than countries with colder climates, such as Canada, Sweden and the USA. One of my German friends said the coldest winter he has spent was in Australia, not because of how low the outside temperature gets, but because of how cold and poorly-build our homes are.

Thermal resilience is achieved when the inside environment of the home is less affected by the changing temperature of the outside environment. This can be done through a quality building envelope. For example, an electric urn must draw a constant flow of electricity to keep water hot, while a thermos that is insulated and airtight can keep water hot for longer without a constant heating source. While thermal control is lower on the priority list when it comes to the building envelope, it's still important. Thermal control measures include variables such as thermal bridges, high-quality windows and doors, and mechanical ventilation.

Thermal bridges

A thermal bridge, also known as a cold bridge or heat bridge, is an important consideration in the design and construction of energy-efficient buildings. It is, essentially, a gap or conductive material that penetrates the thermal envelope, allowing energy (heat) to move freely between the inside and outside of the building. Thermal bridges can occur where two building elements meet, such as at corners, roof/wall junctions or floor/wall junctions. Thermal bridges can cause a range of issues. To ensure the best possible outcomes for energy efficiency, it is important to accurately design, detail and execute a plan for eliminating thermal bridges. This may involve using insulation, adding air sealing and carefully selecting materials to minimise the impact of thermal bridges on the overall thermal envelope of the building.

High-quality windows, doors and skylights

Windows, doors and skylights are considered to be holes in the building's thermal envelope and have to be selected and detailed carefully. They need to provide weather protection, air tightness, thermal insulation, connection to the outdoor environment, egress and architectural aesthetics. As an example, double-glazed or triple-glazed windows work by creating a barrier between the inside and outside of your home. They consist of multiple panes of glass separated by a gap which is filled with an insulating gas. The gap helps to reduce the amount of heat transferred between the inside and outside. Double-glazed and triple-glazed windows can also help to reduce outside noise.

Building Envelope Commissioning Checklist

In the Dream Home Journal, there are checklists to share with your designer and builder. By using this checklist, you can ensure that your home's building envelope is designed and installed correctly, and that it provides optimal energy efficiency and performance. You can get a copy of the Dream Home Journal at **www.lukedavies.co/dreamhomejournal**.

Passivhaus Standard

Passivhaus is a performance-based building standard, used to create high-performance homes. It offers a set of design and performance criteria applicable across any climate zone and architectural style.

The Passivhaus Standard go beyond energy efficiency, analysing factors such as comfort, hygiene, airtightness, indoor air quality and heating demand, all contextualised to the local climate. The principles date to the early 1970s when, under the pressure of rising energy costs caused by an oil crisis, countries such as Denmark, Germany and the USA started to design buildings with lots of insulation, using passive design principles to help reduce the energy and cost it would take to heat a building.

During this acceleration of technological developments, they made lots of mistakes. German homes designed during this period had water leaks because the designers hadn't factored in an adequate water control layer within the structure. In an attempt to solve the problem, external building wrap was installed in the walls and roof to stop leaks. This in turn resulted in mould accumulation, as the wrap wasn't vapour permeable. To fix this, eave and ridge vents were added for ventilation to help move the air and moisture out of the assembly. This resulted in windwashing, air moving past the thermal layer and a 50% loss in insulation performance. To combat this, the cavity was filled with insulation, which, of course, caused an effect similar to one my family and I have experienced when camping in a cheap tent and water leaked inside due to the insulation touching the wrap – the tent effect. As a last-ditch effort to ensure thermal comfort, internal vapour control layers had to be added to stop all moisture from entering the building assembly. Unfortunately, Tasmania is currently making the same mistakes as we increase our homes' insulation and air tightness to reduce energy costs for heating.

There's a way out of this cascade of events, though. Over the past forty years the Passivhaus Standard has evolved, and it's all to do with understanding the building envelope. Today Passivhaus homes, libraries, schools and hospitals have been built and certified all over the world. Passivhaus is a detailed international benchmark which is administered by the Passivhaus Institut.[37] Some places, like Germany and New York, have Passivhaus Standard as their base building code and other places, such as Canada, have set a target to have all new homes meet their Passivhaus Standard by 2050.

The Passivhaus Standard provides performance-based limits for heating demand, cooling demand, primary energy demand, air tightness and summer comfort. To achieve acceptable performance in these areas, the Passivhaus Standard works with five key strategies:

1. High-quality thermal insulation
2. Absence of thermal bridges
3. High-quality windows and doors
4. Air tightness
5. High indoor air quality via MVHR

TECHNOLOGY

If you decide to build to Passivhaus Standard, you will be on the lookout for three different types of certifications:

1. **Building:** A new building or a retrofit can be certified as a Passivhaus.
2. **Components:** An individual product or component like a window or ventilation system can receive Passivhaus certification.
3. **Professional:** A designer, consultant or tradesperson can receive Passivhaus certification. For example, I am a certified Passivhaus tradesperson.

Certified Passivhaus buildings have shown a 90% reduction in energy consumption compared to the average home, and/or a 75% to 80% reduction compared to new homes built to the current NCC standards (2019).

The cost of Passivhaus

While it does cost more to build to Passivhaus Standard, when comparing the cost, you need to also consider the life-cycle cost of the building and the motivations for building, such as comfort, health and sustainability. There are two main areas where the Passivhaus Standard creates cost savings over and above the 2019 NCC. These are:

1. **Heating and cooling systems:** Home builders have upfront savings from purchasing a smaller heating and cooling system in a house that has adhered to the Passivhaus Standard. Home builders have reduced ongoing energy consumption that accrues over time. For example, in a house built to the NCC you will likely need a 15 kilowatt heating and cooling system. In contrast, research estimates that a building that adheres to Passivhaus Standard can be sufficiently cooled or heated using only a 3 kilowatt system. That's five times less energy required in a house built to Passivhaus Standard than a NCC standard home.

2. **Renewable energy systems to meet net zero:** Passivhaus home builders see their energy generation requirements reduced by a factor of three. Using the same maths as above, if you need a 15 kilowatt system to reach net zero for a home built to the NCC, a 5 kilowatt array will meet net zero if you build to Passivhaus Standard.

These reductions mean that over time less money is spent on generating the electricity required to power these systems.

Good design can make the Passivhaus Standard more cost-effective. From concept to construction, optimising architectural design is a major factor in obtaining cost-efficient, high-performing buildings, and thinking about orientation, window placement and shading will help with cost-effectiveness. Even without building to Passivhaus Standard, simply through using an advanced building envelope construction, you can still reduce your heat loss by 70–80%, resulting in a 75–95% reduction in the demand for heating and cooling.

While the NCC does not guarantee thermal comfort, Passivhaus does. Passivhaus accepts only windows that can provide an internal average temperature of 17 degrees Celsius at the glass, taking into account the climate and the external design temperature. If the internal air is 21 degrees Celsius, but you are sitting next to a window with a low internal surface temperature, your body will still feed cold or uncomfortable from the cold surface.

Evaluating performance

By creating a 'digital twin' of the building and conducting computer modelling in the design phase, we can predict how a building will perform for energy efficiency. A 'performance gap' is the difference between computer modelling and the building performance achieved once the building is completed. A gap is common when building high-performance buildings that do not follow strict modelling and high-quality assurance in construction. A performance gap is usually due to one of these factors:

- A lack of accuracy in the simulation software model

- A lack of communication about the level of detail from architect to builder and contractors

- A builder who doesn't understand the importance of the airtight details of Passivhaus design

- A builder who doesn't have the skill required to complete these details to a high standard

- Occupants who don't understand how to live in and use a high-performance building to get the most out of it

Using Passivhaus performance criteria ensures the performance gap is almost non-existent. As a builder, I like the Passivhaus Standard because it minimises building defects, callbacks, warranty work and the risk of future structural problems.

Energy use and energy-saving techniques

Managing ongoing energy use will also have an impact on both the environment and your pocket. Many of the choices you make during construction, especially in terms of energy generation and use, can help reduce greenhouse emissions and your monthly bill.

The size of your home is a key determinant of its environmental impact. Not only does it take more materials to build a large house, but it will also create more carbon dioxide emissions and consume more money to heat, cool and maintain it. It's worth considering spending money on better design and energy efficiency rather than bigger heating and cooling systems.

These days there is a huge range of options around how to provide energy to your home, including solar panels, wind turbines, hydropower, wood heaters, gas and commercial electricity supplies. In many places you can feed the clean energy you generate on-site back into the grid for credits on your power bill.

There are also many ways you can reduce your energy requirements through smart design. As we've already seen, you can use Passivhaus Standard to drastically reduce your energy requirements. You can also reduce your power requirements by choosing low-energy appliances.

Heating systems

The large majority of our energy consumption and cost is driven by heating and cooling. As well as the techniques for thermal control in the building envelope discussed above, there are considerations you can make to achieve optimal heating. The most popular heating options in Australia include the following:

- **Gas-ducted heating systems** work by heating air in a central unit and distributing it through ducts to vents in each room. They are efficient, fast and cost-effective to run. They are also relatively low-maintenance and can last up to twenty years. It is worth noting that some gas energy is phased out in some states of Australia.

- **Electric heating systems** include electric heaters, electric panel heaters and electric radiant heaters. They are easy to install and cost-effective to purchase, but they can be expensive to run and they may not be the most energy-efficient option available.

- **Hydronic heating systems** use hot water to heat the home. They work by circulating hot water through pipes under the floor or through radiators mounted on the walls. Hydronic heating can be ideal for people with allergies or asthma, as it doesn't circulate dust or allergens.

- **Reverse-cycle air conditioning systems** work by absorbing heat from the air outside and transferring it inside to heat your home. Reverse-cycle air conditioners are called heat pumps in Tasmania.

- **Wood heaters** are a renewable heating source and can create a cosy atmosphere, but they can be expensive to install and maintain and they require a constant supply of wood to operate.

- **Solar heating systems** work by capturing the sun's rays and transferring them to a heat storage system which can be used to heat the home. Solar heating is an energy-efficient option, but it can be expensive to install and may not be suitable for all homes.

Another key consideration is the ease of upgrade. Some things, such as kitchen benchtops or appliances, are easy to upgrade, while windows and doors are much harder. There is more long-term value in installing higher-quality windows and other contributions to the building envelope than a higher-quality oven or cupboard.

Smart homes

Building is more than just an action to ensure housing – building itself is belief in the future. Imagine a home that seamlessly blends with its surroundings, its design inspired by the intricate patterns and efficient systems found in nature. Biomimicry, the practice of emulating nature's genius, will guide the creation of sustainable materials and building methods. Think self-healing walls that mimic living organisms, regulating temperature and air quality, or roofs that collect and purify rainwater, contributing to a closed-loop water cycle.

But innovation extends beyond mere mimicry. The home of the future could quite literally be grown, with building components crafted from mycelium, the root structure of mushrooms, or even living structures that integrate plants directly into the walls for insulation, air filtration, and even food production.

Imagine stepping out on to your rooftop garden to receive a package delivered by drone, your garage transformed into a flexible space for work or play, no longer needed for a self-driving car. Nanotechnology will infuse with surfaces: self-cleaning countertops and floors, water-resistant walls that gleam in the sunlight, and fabrics that purify the air you breathe.

An intricate network of sensors will weave through your home, discreetly monitoring your health and the home itself. Sleep patterns, air quality, even subtle shifts in humidity – all tracked and analysed to create a living environment perfectly tailored to your needs. Imagine a home that adjusts the lighting to mimic natural daylight patterns, optimising your circadian rhythm for restful sleep or boosting energy levels.

The future of entertainment will be equally transformative. Spatial computing will allow us to manipulate digital information and environments with intuitive gestures, seamlessly blending the physical and virtual worlds.

Yet, technology will be seamlessly integrated, never intrusive. A high-speed, low-impact network will provide connectivity throughout your home, allowing you to control the environment, access entertainment and communicate with loved ones. But with the simple touch of a button, you can disconnect completely, finding solace in the serenity of your surroundings.

Your dream home won't just be a dwelling; it will be a dynamic, evolving ecosystem that enhances your life in ways you never thought possible.

Imagine a world where the limitations of ageing are pushed back. Scientists are exploring groundbreaking research that hints at the possibility of dramatically extending human lifespans. This exciting frontier in science could lead to homes designed not just for decades, but for centuries of vibrant living, adapting to the evolving needs of their inhabitants.

DREAM HOME-WORK

Ensure you are aware of the latest developments in sustainable technology before committing to a design. Modern developments can save you money not only during the build but also in the future by lowering your energy bill and your maintenance costs and increasing the lifespan of your home.

Look for ways to make your home more sustainable (and reduce your costs) through designing in-line with high-performance principles or Passivhaus Standard and ensuring you have a high-quality building envelope.

Ensure you have researched the latest developments in materials, energy systems and building technology to future-proof your home.

Check out these online resources:

Australian Government Your Home Guide to Environmentally Sustainable Homes: www.yourhome.gov.au

World Green Building Council: www.worldgbc.org/thecommitment

APR Building Services' Energy Smart Housing: www.aprbuildingservices.com.au/C1_Energy_Smart_Housing.html

Overarching technology statement

Where in your dream home design could you implement high-quality and high-tech design or materials to improve your home build? Are you planning to implement the Passivhaus Standard? Will you generate all your own electricity with a solar system?

Write this down in your Dream Home Journal.

You should now have six overarching statements on your Dream Home Journal. This is a useful tool to share with your design team to give an indication of your priorities and values.

Summary

In this chapter we've looked at ways to use Passivhaus Standard and high-performance principles to create a sturdy building envelope which will reduce your energy consumption and your ongoing impact on the environment while still taking your health and comfort into consideration. We've also looked at ways to reduce your energy consumption and some of the technological innovations that are transforming building design and construction.

It costs more to construct a home to Passivhaus Standard than by simply meeting the requirements of the NCC, but every home builder must come to their own decision around whether it's worth the extra cost.

For some people, a high-performing building envelope is worth more than more cosmetic features such as stone benchtops and high-end internal finishes. Passivhaus heating and cooling systems can be up to five times smaller than in a conventional building, so there are significant savings to be made (alongside the lower environmental impacts). If it comes to making the hard choice, I would rather have a great, well-insulated window than a granite benchtop or large expensive tub.

9
Our Home, Planet Earth

We all share one dream home: the planet Earth. Underpinning all the decisions you are going to make in the Six Elements of home design is the knowledge that we, as a global society, are currently living through an ecological and climate crisis.

Unfortunately, a lot of the construction industry is still in the dark about what's happening with the planet's ecosystems. As a builder, conscious of the danger our planet is in, I can see a future that doesn't look promising if we continue on our current trajectory. We're in a climate crisis and have a limited window of opportunity in which to act. We should be acting right now. Not leaving it to somebody else. Not waiting another five years. It's our responsibility. It's got to be today.

In this chapter I'll share some of the arguments that put me on a path towards sustainable building and finding solutions in my industry to the climate crisis. I can now confidently say I offer my clients building alternatives that will dramatically decrease the impact of their homes on the environment both during construction and into the future.

Human impact

It took 250,000 years for the human population to reach 1 billion people, which happened in the early 1800s. It took just 125 years to reach 2 billion. In less than 100 years, we have now reached 8 billion. Will our planet support so many people? What type of homes do we need to build to support our planet? How is this sustainable?

There was one single graph that changed my mind on the climate crisis, which was presented in the Netflix documentary *Breaking Boundaries*. It showed the fluctuations in Earth's temperature before the Holocene – the name geologists use for the last 10,000 years – which would vary plus and minus 10 degrees Celsius in a decade.[38] The temperature stabilised only 10,000 years ago, at the beginning of a remarkable period when the planet's temperature varied only plus or minus 1 degrees Celsius. This is what enabled and created the world we know today. Sea levels stayed stable and, for the first time, we had predictable seasons. This is when humans started building modern civilisation.

The first migration of fully modern humans out of Africa was around 90,000 years ago, Aboriginal people arrived in Australia around 60,000 years ago, and the beginning of agriculture was only 10,000 years ago, shortly after swinging temperatures stabilised and we had the first predictable seasons. Humans began to grow food soon after, and a few millennia later great European civilisations like the Greeks and Romans began to develop. All this was made possible by the stable temperatures enjoyed by the planet.

In the last few hundred years, levels of atmospheric carbon dioxide changed dramatically at the advent of the Industrial Revolution. For millennia, levels of carbon dioxide fluctuated in the atmosphere but they never exceeded 300 parts per million. Around 1950 they shot through this barrier and have been rapidly increasing ever since. Today they are around 415 parts per million.

This is because today we are digging up decomposing animals and plants and burning them as fossil fuels all at once and in a short period of time. This releases unprecedented levels of carbon dioxide into the atmosphere and we produce enormous amounts of waste while we do it.

In his book *A Life on Our Planet*, David Attenborough offers us his 'witness statement', providing three statistics – world population, parts per million of carbon dioxide in the atmosphere and percentage of worldwide wilderness – to show how the planet has changed over his lifetime. In 1937, when Attenborough was a boy, the stats were: 2.3 billion people, 280 parts per million of carbon dioxide in the atmosphere and 66% remaining wilderness. Today, only eighty-seven years later, we're at 8 billion people, 415 parts per million of carbon dioxide, with only 35% of natural wilderness left.[39]

In a single lifetime, humans have warmed the planet more than 1 degree Celsius. We are just leaving the most stable period the planet has ever seen and entering what scientists call the Anthropocene, a period where humans are responsible for the change in the planet's temperature.[40,41]

It's a bit like sick building syndrome that is impacting our homes, only this building is much, much bigger and much, much more sick. The carbon dioxide emissions and waste we are producing to build and run our homes has hidden effects, and it has contributed to a sick planet syndrome. We now know that climate change and disruptions to Earth's natural ecosystems are having profound impacts on health.[42] To respond to this growing public health threat, *The Lancet* Commission launched their international, multidisciplinary health collaboration: *The Lancet Countdown on Health and Climate Change*, which publishes annual reports on the health impacts of climate change. Its eighth iteration, the 2023 report, contains contributions by fourteen scientists from fifty-two separate agencies.

This report showed that those who are susceptible to the health impacts of heatwaves (those older than sixty-five and those younger than one) 'are now exposed to twice as many heatwave days as they would have experienced in 1986–2005'. The total global land area affected by drought has risen from 18% (1951–1960) to 47% (in 2013–2022).[43] With almost half of our global land susceptible to drought, it is even more important we know how to build homes that are healthy for us, and healthy for the planet.

Bill Gates says there are only two numbers you need to know about the climate disaster and that's 51 billion and zero – 51 billion tonnes of greenhouse gases is what the world typically adds to the atmosphere every year. Zero (greenhouse gases) is what we must aim for.[44]

Another compelling set of data is the projections for what will happen to global temperatures if we don't act. Researchers suggest that if we do nothing, the temperature could rise by 3.6–7.2 degrees Celsius by 2100. The difference in global temperatures is put into perspective by author and Intergovernmental Panel on Climate Change scientist Joelle Gergis in her book *Humanity's Moment*. In her captivating work, she explains that by looking at temperatures on Earth previously, we can see that, 'even between 1.5 and 2°C of warming will trigger huge reconfigurations of the planet's climate system'. She continues by stating that the Greenland and West Antarctic ice sheets will be 'lost almost completely and irreversibly over thousands of years' if we have sustained warming levels between 2°C and 3°C. She predicts that the planet will become 'unrecognisable between 3°C and 4°C' and that 'the Earth as we once knew it will no longer exist.'[45]

If we *do* act, we may be able to keep temperatures at the levels we saw in 2020. We need to act now to prevent exponential problems in the future. We are acting on climate change not only to 'save our planet'. The planet will survive no matter what. Life will continue with us or without us. What we have to do is protect our species and all the other species that we have now become responsible for.

Our journey as a species began billions of years ago with the first single-celled organisms. Through the remarkable process of evolution, life diversified and complexified, eventually giving rise to us humans. We often view ourselves as separate from nature, even a destructive force upon it. But our very existence is a testament to our deep connection with the natural world, woven into the intricate web of life.

In fact, our bodies are home to ecosystems more diverse and complex than many of Earth's most celebrated natural wonders. The human microbiome, the trillions of microorganisms that inhabit our gut and other parts of our bodies, represents an evolutionary marvel, showcasing the interconnectedness of all living things. We carry within us a microcosm of the planet's biodiversity, a reminder that we are not just inhabitants of Earth, but living expressions of its intricate web of life.

This perspective challenges us to rethink our role. We are not simply residents of this planet; we are active participants in its ongoing evolution. As stewards of Earth, we have a responsibility to build homes and communities that support both human flourishing and the health of our natural world.

Zero waste habitat

A zero waste habitat embodies the principle of maximising the value your home creates for you and the planet, while eliminating or minimising waste in all its forms – from carbon emissions and energy consumption to materials, water, space, time, effort and even wasted ideas. Our planet possesses abundant resources, but we often squander them through inefficient practices and unsustainable choices. So, let's look at each of these in more detail.

Wasted emissions

The hierarchy of managing carbon dioxide emissions is to 'build nothing, build less, build clever and build efficiently.'[46] When we do build, achieving zero emissions means looking at your carbon footprint. According to the United Nations Environment Programme, the construction sector is responsible for 39% of global human carbon dioxide emissions, while in Australia nearly 25% of greenhouse gas emissions come from the construction and use of buildings. As an industry, we must act to reduce our carbon footprint – there's no point in building beautiful homes for people if they damage our greater home – Earth. A way to lower your environmental impact is to offset your construction emissions; it's not the solution, but it helps. My company offsets our carbon emissions for all our projects by planting trees, and we're on track to reach our goal of one million trees. There are many organisations around the world that will help you offset your emissions by planting trees or using other carbon sequestration initiatives.

Unfortunately, calculating the carbon footprint of a new home is not a simple task, though increasingly the industry is working to address this. The different types of carbon dioxide emissions you need to consider are:

- **Embodied carbon:** First, you must consider the embodied carbon in your choice of construction materials. This includes how the raw materials are sourced, such as through mining or forestry, how they are transported to the manufacturing facilities and how they are processed into building materials, such as through smelting or casting.

We know that the production of some materials, such as steel, has a high carbon cost, while others, such as timber, can sequester carbon dioxide as they grow. Needless to say, if you choose to use repurposed, upcycled or salvaged building materials, rather than purchasing materials new, the embodied carbon in your home construction will be dramatically reduced. The materials that contain the highest levels of embodied carbon are concrete, masonry, plastic and steel.

- **Construction carbon:** Second, you must consider the carbon cost for the construction itself, including the way the materials, and the builders, are transported to the construction site, and the energy used to prepare the site, connect services and assemble the building. Each one of these processes releases carbon dioxide emissions that contributes to the building's carbon footprint. In addition, there is the 'carbon overhead' of running the businesses that make all these processes possible. Building materials are heavy and require a huge amount of energy to transport. Choosing locally manufactured materials will drastically reduce the impact of transporting materials to your site.

- **Operational carbon:** Third, you must consider the ongoing carbon footprint of using the building throughout its lifespan. This is the operational carbon footprint and includes the energy the building will use – for example, heating and cooling. Operational carbon also includes the end-of-life disposal of the construction materials. The carbon footprint of the building's operational use can be dramatically reduced through smart design techniques (such as Passivhaus), choosing renewable power and choosing materials that either are biodegradable or can be reused or repurposed at the end of the building's life-cycle. Over the life-cycle of a building, up to 80% of the carbon dioxide emissions it produces is operational carbon. This makes operational carbon redesign the low-hanging fruit that will make the biggest and quickest impact on reducing carbon emissions.

Wasted energy

The energy we use in our home has a huge impact on our carbon footprint and the planet. We're aiming for buildings to have zero energy consumption.

According to the Australian Bureau of Statistics, in 1999 about 45% of houses were between twenty and fifty years old, with 18% fifty years or older.[47] Older buildings are poorly insulated, they have single-glazed windows and they use a lot of energy. They will continue to require more electricity to operate, and new buildings can help offset this by incorporating better design and producing more power than they need to supply renewable power back to the power grid. The minimum standard I'd like to see when building new homes is zero energy consumption. If possible, we should build to compensate for older houses too.

Wasted material

There are 27 million tonnes of waste created in Australia every year from construction and demolition, and that's 44% of all waste in Australia. Technological developments are making small improvements in this area by making prefabrication processes that were once viable only for modular (kit) homes available for custom-build designs.

In a conventional build, large bundles of timber are transported to a building location and manually cut to size on-site, which creates a lot of waste and offcuts which must be transported to landfills. It's now possible, however, to measure and pre-cut timber in a factory to precisely fit a customised design. This means that only the necessary materials are transported to the site, the factory has the potential to be powered by renewable energy, and offcuts can be dedicated to other projects from the factory so less material goes to landfill. This will become increasingly possible for other building materials, such as cladding, sheeting and roofing.

All materials in a building can be considered in the building life-cycle. A material can either be recycled at the end of building or it can't. The materials that can't end up in landfill. The goal is not to have any material waste that ends up in landfill, we want to re-use, re-purpose or re-cycle. On an average building site we take about ten tandem trailer loads of new material off-cut to our local waste centre. I imagine a world without construction waste because waste is ultimately caused by inefficient design. The construction industry must move from the linear economy of extract > manufacture > use > waste, to a circular economy of extract > manufacture > use > back to use or manufacture, making our building resources infinite.

When selecting your materials, ask your design team: 'What is the building material life-cycle?' and 'Can the material be reused or recycled in the future, can it be composted or will it go to landfill?' Ask your builder how they are managing waste on-site and if they have bins with compartments to keep materials separate for recycling and composting.

Another form of waste to consider is your ongoing household waste. How will you dispose of your waste? Your options include:

- **Rubbish bins:** These will go to landfill or incineration, which is not ideal. Try to minimise what goes in this bin, which starts when you are buying things.
- **Recycling:** This can include repurposing, mending and upcycling.

- **Compost:** This means reusing organic waste in the garden.

Wasted water

Water is our planet's lifeblood that sustains all living things. While it may seem abundant, clean and accessible, water is a finite and precious resource. We must treat it with respect and prioritise its conservation, especially in our homes, where it's easy to take water for granted.

Every drop counts. Wasted water isn't just about leaky taps; it's about the entire life-cycle of water in your home. During construction, vast amounts of water are often used for various processes. In the future, we'll see a shift towards smarter building practices that conserve water. Rainwater harvesting systems will become commonplace, capturing and storing precipitation for use on-site. On-site water recycling systems will ensure that wastewater is treated and reused for tasks like irrigation, further minimising environmental impact.

Inside your home, water efficiency will be a core design principle. Low-flow fixtures will deliver ample water for everyday needs while significantly reducing consumption. Greywater systems will repurpose gently used water from showers and laundry for flushing toilets or watering gardens. Smart appliances will monitor water usage and detect leaks, helping you identify areas for improvement.

By making conscious choices and embracing innovative technologies, you can significantly reduce your home's water footprint. This not only benefits the environment but also lowers your utility bills and contributes to a more sustainable future for all. Remember, every drop saved matters. Let's create homes that celebrate water as the precious resource it is.

Wasted space

Space, both within and surrounding our homes, is a precious resource that deserves mindful consideration. Wasted space—whether in the form of sprawling urban development, oversized houses, or inefficiently designed interiors—represents a missed opportunity to create truly sustainable and fulfilling living environments.

On a macro level, sprawling urban development contributes to habitat destruction, increased transportation needs and a greater reliance on infrastructure. By prioritising compact, walkable communities and utilising existing urban spaces creatively, we can reduce our environmental footprint and foster a sense of connection and belonging.

Similarly, the size of our homes matters. A smaller footprint not only translates to fewer materials used and less waste generated during construction but also reduces the ongoing energy consumption required for heating, cooling and maintenance. Designing homes that prioritise function and efficiency, while still providing ample space for occupants' needs and desires, is key to achieving this balance.

Internally, wasted space can take many forms. Poorly designed layouts, awkward room shapes and excessive circulation areas can all lead to inefficient use of square metreage. By employing thoughtful design principles and incorporating flexible, multi-functional spaces, we can create homes where every square metre serves a purpose and contributes to the overall well-being of the occupants.

By carefully considering our needs and lifestyle, we can design homes that maximise space, eliminate wasted space and maximise the potential of every square metre.

Wasted potential

The construction of a dream home involves a symphony of creativity, collaboration and problem-solving. However, amidst this complex process lies the most impactful waste of all: wasted potential. It encompasses not just the tangible resources we squander but also the invaluable human element – the skills, knowledge and innovative thinking of everyone involved in the project. Wasted potential can manifest in various forms, hindering the realisation of a truly fulfilling and efficient home.

One of the most critical wastes of potential arises from untapped creativity and ideas. When consultants, experts or team members aren't empowered to contribute their unique skills and perspectives, or when valuable insights are overlooked, we miss out on opportunities for innovation and optimisation. Information should flow in a single direction without coming back on itself; this is why it's crucial to engage experts early in the process, fostering an environment where ideas flow freely and collaborative problem-solving thrives.

Another significant form of wasted potential lies in inefficient processes that lead to overprocessing, rework, excessive motion and waiting. These issues not only squander time and resources but also create frustration, disrupt project flow and increase transaction costs. By streamlining communication, clearly defining roles and responsibilities, and utilising collaborative tools and technologies, we can minimise these inefficiencies and ensure a smoother, more productive building experience.

Ultimately, wasted potential can hinder the creation of a truly exceptional home. By recognising and addressing these challenges, we can unlock the full potential of every dream home project. This means not just building beautiful and functional homes but also creating a positive and fulfilling experience for everyone involved, from the initial design concept to the final handover of keys. The goal is to build a home that embodies the essence of its occupants, reflects their values, and nurtures their well-being, all while minimising waste and maximising efficiency.

The future of construction calculation

While it is difficult, it's also critical that as an industry we get to grips with not only calculating monetary costs but also calculating carbon emission, energy use and waste.

Here's our end goal: imagine you get a set of plans drawn up and you are given four numbers. The first is an accurate construction price for your home because all the materials are individually priced according to quantity. The second is an accurate carbon cost of your home, with all materials and calculation of operational costs itemised in the same way. The third is an accurate estimate of energy use to run your home per year. The fourth is a number on how much waste your home will produce during its construction. With rapid advancement in AI, it won't be long and we'll have design software that will calculate the material price and carbon cost automatically and will update with changes. This means that every time you draw in a window, or change the shape of a window, or choose a new material, the software recalculates, and every time you draw in a concrete slab, or add a tap or a particular oven or a door handle, you have a carbon dioxide emissions number and a price, which are totalled up for your whole home design – making it easy to make real-time decisions.

As more people ask questions about zero emissions, zero energy and zero material waste the industry will be forced to respond. I encourage you to ask these questions of your design team and challenge the team and yourself to work in the direction of building a zero-waste habitat for your dream home.

Sustainability plus regenerative design

In an age of growing environmental awareness, 'sustainability' has become a buzzword. But what does it truly mean in the context of building our dream homes? Sustainability is about ensuring our actions today don't compromise the needs of future generations. It's about minimising our impact and preserving resources. But to truly achieve a sustainable future, we must go beyond simply doing less harm and actively seek to improve the environment. This is where regenerative design comes in.

Regenerative design enhances sustainability. While sustainability focuses on minimising negative impacts, regenerative design actively seeks to restore and regenerate. It's about creating homes that give back to the environment and our communities. This might involve generating more energy than is consumed, restoring natural ecosystems and using materials that improve over time.

This shift in mindset from sustainability to include regeneration requires a fundamental shift in our thinking. It's about moving from a fear of scarcity to a belief in abundance. A scarcity mindset limits our vision, leading us to focus solely on reducing consumption and making do with existing resources. It can trap us in a cycle of incremental improvements, hindering true innovation.

Consider the story of Henry Ford and the Model T. If Ford had solely focused on sustainability with a scarcity mindset, he might have simply tried to make horse-drawn carriages more efficient. Instead, he embraced an abundance mindset, envisioning a future where cars were affordable and accessible to everyone. This led to the revolutionary assembly line and mass production, transforming transportation and society itself.

An abundance mindset opens up a world of possibilities. It allows us to imagine bold solutions, explore new technologies and create homes that not only minimise their impact, but also actively contribute to a healthier planet. With an abundance mindset, we can envision entirely new building systems, materials that regenerate over time, and homes that seamlessly integrate with the natural world.

Minimising waste, as we learned in the previous chapter, is a key part of this equation. By reducing waste in all its forms – materials, energy, water, time and even human potential – we create homes that are not only beautiful and functional but also contribute to a healthier, more vibrant planet.

Other design principles explained

Clients often ask me about the difference between passive solar principles, net zero principles and Passivhaus Standard for the purpose of building a environment-positive home. Below is an outline of these and other design approaches:

- **Passive solar** sounds a lot like Passivhaus, but it's not the same thing. Passive solar design focuses on solar heat gains to reduce heating costs, and primarily looks at the placement of windows to get more sun into the building. Passive solar is often used with thermal mass to absorb heat into a concrete floor or a masonry wall through the day, which will then release heat through the night. There are no standards for how much sun should be let into a building to achieve passive solar. The downside is that you can't control the sun or the clouds, which means it can easily get too hot or not hot enough, particularly when it's overcast or when the sun goes down. Many passive solar homes can overheat in late summer and early autumn and are too cold in late autumn and early winter, and passive solar design does not address moisture-driven damage, indoor air quality or thermal comfort for people living in the building.

- **Net zero** describes a building that can produce more energy over a one-year period than it consumes. Net zero design often uses photovoltaic (PV, or solar) panels to offset energy use by creating an equal amount of energy as the building consumes. A poorly constructed building can achieve net zero if it has sufficient solar panels to feed its energy demands. Like passive solar design, net zero principles do not necessarily need to consider the occupants' health and comfort or the quality of internal air.

- **Nationwide House Energy Rating Scheme (NatHERS)** is a star rating measuring energy efficiency for homes. NatHERS uses software to assess the star rating of your home, although this software can easily be manipulated by changing the name of a room. For example, if you change the name of a bedroom to a store room without changing anything physical on the design, you can achieve a different star rating. This is not the best way to ensure a building is energy-efficient. The rating also does not consider the health and comfort of the occupants – the main reason to build a building.

- **The Living Building Challenge** is considered the most rigorous green building certification in the world and represents the highest level of sustainable design and construction. It challenges architects, builders and designers to create buildings that actively regenerate and improve the surrounding environment. The certification criteria include strict standards for energy and water usage, indoor air quality, materials selection and social equity. To achieve certification, a building must operate for at least twelve months with net zero energy and water usage and meet a host of other sustainability criteria.

- **The Green Star rating system**, developed by the Green Building Council of Australia (GBCA), is a comprehensive sustainability certification program for commercial buildings. GBCA has developed a rating system for homes called Green Star homes. The rating system sets a new benchmark for sustainable residential buildings, promoting environmentally responsible, healthy and comfortable living spaces. It encourages builders and developers to embrace sustainable design and construction practices.

- **A High-Performance building** can only truly be deemed 'high-performance' if it not only adheres to rigorous design principles but also undergoes meticulous testing and modelling throughout both the design and construction phases. This comprehensive approach ensures that the building's energy efficiency, airtightness, thermal comfort, and indoor air quality are not merely theoretical aspirations but actual, measurable outcomes. From initial energy modelling to on-site blower door tests and thermal imaging, a high-performance building is a testament to the fusion of scientific understanding and skilled craftsmanship, resulting in a living environment that excels in both comfort and sustainability.

CASE STUDY: The Green Village and Green School

I visited the Green Village in Bali (www.greenvillagebali.com) and the nearby Green School (www.greenschool.org). Although not suitable for Tasmania, they are fantastic examples of low-impact building techniques. Everything in their buildings is made of bamboo, including roofs, walls, floors and furniture. These projects were dreamed up by John and Cynthia Hardy, designed by architecture company Ibuku and built using traditional Balinese construction techniques.

Bamboo is one of the most sustainable construction materials on the planet. As well as being incredibly flexible and adaptable, it has a strength equivalent to steel. Bamboo is a renewable resource – the growing process sequesters carbon and the bamboo used in the construction of one home can be regrown in just four years. It's also grown in the local area, which reduces transport costs. At the Green Village and Green School, the bamboo is treated with borax – a natural salt solution that removes sugar and makes it inedible for insects. This can increase the lifespan of the buildings to 100 years. When the buildings do reach the end of their lives, they will compost back into the soil with minimal environmental impact.

Summary

This chapter has looked at the urgency for change faced by life on this planet. The good news is that by building a dream home, you are undertaking a project that can make a positive contribution to improving our planet's problems. Environmental impacts will only change if we do.

PART THREE
UNDERSTANDING THE INDUSTRY

The journey to building your dream home can be bumpy or smooth – all depending on the way the project is managed from the start. You want the ride to be as smooth and enjoyable as possible so that you, like me, can enjoy the building process as much as the finished home.

There are three principles I use for every project I undertake, but they work *especially* well for one of the biggest projects of your life: building the home of your dreams. The principles are:

Principle 1: Have a clear plan and know your intended outcome. Having clarity is power. Knowing your goal will make you more likely to achieve it. Once you've worked through Part III, you'll have a much clearer understanding of your plan and you'll have the tools to brief your design team to achieve your outcome.

Principle 2: Use the best tools and methods. Design and construct is the best method of building an architectural home, but we'll take a look at all the construction options in Chapter 10, and in Chapter 13 and 14 we'll look at some of the tools I find essential to the smooth running of a construction project.

Principle 3: Align the best team. Choosing the right builder, architect and other specialists, such as the interior designer, contractors and landscape architects, is critical to the success of your project. They need to work together at key decision-making points. In Chapter 11 and 12 we'll review how to bring together the best team to build your dream home.

10
Home Construction Options

There is an array of options for home construction, all of which can lead to different outcomes and project costs. Most of these come down to the trade-off and tension between certainty and flexibility. In this chapter we'll take a close look at this tension, as well as the pros and cons of different options for construction: existing house or speculative (spec) home, off-the-plan, standard custom and architectural.

Certainty versus flexibility

Most of us do not have unlimited funds to pour into a home construction project: we need to stay on budget. Custom-building projects are notorious for blowing the budget, however, sometimes by astronomical amounts. For this reason, many people go for options that give them more certainty around the construction costs. This, unfortunately, often means they sacrifice the personal design details and compromise on the Six Elements of a Dream Home.

If you buy a house that's already built, there is a lot of certainty about what you are going to get, but there is limited flexibility around customising it to your unique needs. When you build an architectural home, you have full flexibility to make any choice you like but you have little certainty about what it will look like or what it will cost.

In this equation, most people choose certainty, simply due to human nature and the fear of the unknown. I'd like to propose to you that if you use the D&C methodology, with the right tools and team, you can build a customised home with full flexibility *and* a high degree of certainty. First, let's take a look in detail at each of the options for finding a home.

An existing house

This has a set price tag and complete certainty around what you are buying. You can walk in, take a look, feel the space and decide whether you want to buy it.

The advantage is that you can see what you're getting. The value is easily detectable, whereas with an architectural home design you are provided only with a set of plans and it's hard to visualise the finished product. The disadvantage is that there is zero flexibility and a compromise of your unique vision in the home and likely built without the Six Elements in mind.

Off-the-plan

Off-the-plan homes are created by large construction corporations who are building a large number of houses based on the same plans. These houses offer certainty in pricing.

The construction of these could be through building on-site or prefabricated off-site. Though you may be able to make some adjustments to the design, such as moving certain walls or changing the paint colour, the plans and inclusions are largely set in stone. These homes often have a focus on street appeal and number of rooms, rather than a personalised floor plan and site-specific design and orientation. You can sometimes walk through a pre-built display home so you know what the house will look and feel like.

Standard custom

In a standard custom-built home, you employ a building designer (rather than an architect) to develop your home plans. With this option, you've got full flexibility to do what you want with the design. In most cases, clients will approach a building designer with plans they have sketched up themselves. The building designer will draft these plans into the construction documents for a house, without making many changes or suggestions to the client's design.

Architectural

At the other end of the spectrum there is the architect-designed home. You can make any decision you like because you're starting with a blank piece of paper. I love knowing that we can draw a line, and that line becomes where you dig in the ground and where your walls get built. The sky's the limit. You engage an architect for their experience and creative skills. It's their job to delve deep into your needs, explore the site in detail and provide a response using the full powers of their professional expertise.

Unfortunately, architect-designed homes are notorious for running over budget. After analysing some of our records, I found that 65% of architectural plans that were designed and given to us to quote never got built, not even by another builder. I suspect the likely cause is that the designed house, once quoted, went over the client's allocated budget.

There are three core reasons why the architectural design process for a dream home can go wrong:

HOME CONSTRUCTION OPTIONS

1. A client's brief and their expectations are never discussed symbiotically.

2. There is a lack of training for architects in understanding construction costs and client management so architects feel confident in communicating when a client's ideas will not work. It doesn't matter how good the builder is at quoting if the home is designed over the client's budget.

3. The conventional method is for an architect to design a home with no involvement from the builder.

CASE STUDY: My dream home

When designing my own home, I decided to use an architect for the job. Even though I have over twenty years' experience in building dream homes, and though I will be building the home, I have engaged an architect to design it.

Why did I decide to do this? Yes, I'm great at working with my clients' designs, critiquing them and making them better – but doing my own? For my own home I wanted to be challenged in new ways. I wanted to tell an architect my brief and then see what they produced when they came back to me. I've employed this approach for the entire designing process, and it's resulted in some truly exciting options. I'm building both a cabin *and* a house that I would have never designed myself, and I truly love both designs.

> You hire an architect not simply to draw up the plans in your head but to bring new ideas to your project and to approach your design challenges in ways you'd never come up with yourself.

On-site or off-site?

Building can take place on-site or off-site. Typically, buildings are stick-framed or bricked up on the building site. All the tradespeople involved in the building travel to the site every day to work. Off-site prefabrication building components can be manufactured in modular volumetric, panelised or flat-packed format. Modularity is the future of the construction industry, so understanding this option will be valuable.

A prefabricated volumetric home is built off-site in a factory, where the home is almost completed – including the cladding, the bathrooms and the kitchen sink. Then the completed house is put onto a truck and taken to the site. Larger buildings are joined together once they are placed on-site. Volumetric modules have to be designed to suit the size and weight that a truck is legally allowed to carry on the road.

A panelised home is built off-site in a factory. The floors, walls, ceiling and roof are all made and then put onto a truck and taken to the site to assemble. Panels can be lightweight timber or precast concrete.

Panelising allows for more flexibility for differently shaped building structures. A benefit is the building's shell goes together quickly, so the building becomes watertight in a few weeks.

Off-site prefabrication is used for on-site construction homes. Items like roof trusses, external windows and doors, joinery and other internal components often get made in a factory and delivered to the building site when needed.

The machines are set up to produce building materials in a certain size and shape. You benefit from the economies of scale, but your ability to customise can be constrained.

Design and construction

D&C is a form of architect design where the architect (or a good building designer) and builder work together to develop the design and construct the building. A good D&C company has a continuous improvement process that constantly transfers data and information from architect to builder to architect, making the design of each home better and better. My company works with the D&C model, which we'll look at in Chapter 12. This model offers the best of both certainty and flexibility, enabling a project to be accurately costed from the start and the full flexibility of an architect-designed home.

DREAM HOME-WORK

Decide whether you are going to deal first with an architect or building designer and put your plans out for tender or use the D&C methodology.

Write down how much time per week you want to put in your calendar to manage the process.

Decide on your real budget and what you are going to tell your architect/designer and builder.

Think about your comfort levels around stepping into the unknown. Will you be able to lay down hundreds of thousands of dollars for a house you can't see, touch or experience, or would you rather stick to the certainty of an existing house or display home?

Summary

You can choose the absolute certainty of an existing house or increase your options incrementally by going for an off the plan house. If you are more adventurous, you can have your plans drawn up by a designer for a standard custom-build, or you can go for the blue-sky possibilities of engaging an architect to design your dream home. You open up the flexibility to create a unique home that's tailor-made for your needs, but you also open the possibility of budget blowouts. The solution to this problem? We talk about this in Chapter 12.

11
Building A Team

Projects don't *go* wrong, they *start* wrong, and selecting your team of specialists is probably the most important choice you will make in your home construction journey. When building your dream home, you don't want any random architect or builder, you want a team experienced in creating dream homes and, ideally, a team that has already worked together.

In this chapter I'll give you a quick overview of the key roles you need to fill and the professional consultants you will need to source to complete your dream home project. We'll also take a look at how to go about finding the perfect architect/designer and builder and the questions you should ask.

Roles on a construction project

The homeowner, architect and builder are the three critical roles in a home build, and it is important they have a strong working relationship, but there are many other roles that can be involved in a building project. Let's take a look at each one in detail.

Architect

The role of an architect is to offer you their experience to plan your project. They collect information from a client (a brief) and use that information to design a building.

An architect has been through many years of university training and must be registered. The building plans they produce are detailed and considered and their fees reflect that. The first conversation should start with them asking you a simple question: 'Why are you doing this project?'

The architect controls the whole design process, including creating the main concept design, handling design consultants and managing the process. Sometimes the architect's fee includes allowances for time to help manage the construction project if any decisions need to be made while the home is being constructed. This is well worth the investment, as having the person who created the design available to help with decisions through the build is critical.

If the architect is not involved, you risk the builder or tradespeople making random decisions without any context around the intentions of the architect's design.

Building designer

A building designer has the qualifications to design and draft building plans. Typically, a building designer will draft your design ideas, rather than creatively interpreting the brief. You're likely to get a less considered design and less design details that have been resolved if you approach a building designer.

Often a building designer's business is set up to handle more volume than quality, which means their fees are lower than an architect's. A good building designer can have the same skill and passion as an architect but without the accreditation to call themself an architect. Many of the building designers I know care about their work, but their plans often do not take into consideration all of the Six Elements. There's generally a lack of information on their plans, which leaves a lot of the decisions and interpretations up to the builders and tradespeople working on the building site. This is far from ideal when building your dream home. Some building designers don't engage design consultants – if you hire a building designer, check whether they will handle this or you'll need to source your design consultants separately.

Design consultants & certifiers

A building designer or architect can do only so much in developing your building plans and gaining your building approval. You will also need a team of consultants to take care of specialist areas.

The following is a list of design consultants and assessments you may need:

- **Site surveyor:** They will record the contours of the land, check the boundaries and mark the location of the sewerage point, storm water point, phone connection, power connection and any other features of the block, such as fences or existing buildings. The service can differ between residential sites and rural sites. They can also set out new boundary pegs if needed.

- **Flood inundation, erosion report or sensitive area:** A geotechnical engineer or other specialist may be needed if the site is in a high risk or sensitive area.

- **Land capability assessment:** If you want to build on rural-resource-zoned land, you may need an agronomist to classify the land in terms of its agricultural use and identify possible building sites.

- **Independent planner report:** A consultant to do a planning report for the local council if your development application needs to respond to certain performance criteria.

- **Acting agent:** A consultant helps with the administration and handles the applications to the council and acts on the clients' behalf to liaise with all certificates and permits.

- **Site classification:** A geotechnical engineer will do a soil test that checks the composition of the soil on your block, which will affect the kind of footings that can be used. They also provide the wind speed for your block, which is used to work out the bracing and tie-downs needed in your home.

- **Environmental impact report:** An Environmental Management Plan (EMP) outlines how environmental impacts will be managed and minimised during your home construction project. This plan considers factors such as erosion and sediment control, waste management, noise pollution and protection of native flora and fauna.

- **Bushfire assessment:** If your block is in a bush area, you may need an accredited specialist to assess your BAL and, if necessary, prepare a bushfire management report. This will detail the actions to take in the event of a bushfire and any preparation requirements, such as constructing overpassing bays on your road.

- **Waste water assessment:** If you are building on a block that hasn't been connected to services, you will need a waste water system. This must be designed by an accredited waste water designer.

- **Storm water assessment:** If your block does not have a storm water connection, you will need a storm water assessment to detail how water will run off your roof and stay within your boundary.

- **Passivhaus consultant:** They will assess and examine each stage of the project to ensure the building will meet requirements to become Passivhaus certified.

- **Passivhaus certifier:** A licenced certifier to approve the design for construction and to help certify the building upon completion.

- **Energy rating:** You must obtain an energy rating for your home from an accredited specialist to make sure it meets the minimum 'stars' required.

- **Building surveyor (or certifier):** Once all the documentation has been developed by all design consultants and the engineering and architectural plans are ready, the building surveyor checks and certifies all the documentation before it is submitted to the council. In some cases the building surveyor or certifier can issue the permits without the council. The building surveyor also comes to the site to do the building inspections. They can do five inspections at different stages of construction: the footing inspection (though sometimes the engineer will do this), the frame inspection, the waterproofing inspection, the occupancy inspection and the completion inspection. The building surveyor will check the construction against the building permit details.

- **Plumbing inspector:** They check the plumbing permit details against the plumbing installed on the site.

Structural engineer

The engineer works with the architectural plans and the design consultant reports and plans to make the design work on the building site. After the architect, the engineer does the most work in terms of preparing the documents. They will draft the structure for the building – for example, how the slab or footings will be constructed, based on the soil test, or how the building will be braced, based on the wind load and size of the beams that will be needed. The engineer determines all the structural components of the building.

Once the engineer is finished, there are two sets of plans: an architectural set of documents and a structural engineering set of documents.

Quantity surveyor

A quantity surveyor is often engaged by an architect to provide their clients with a cost estimate on building their design. This is usually a rough estimate, as pricing a construction project depends on a large number of variables, including the specific builders and their location.

Builder

The builder takes the plans developed by the architect or building designer, estimates the cost of building and then constructs the house. The principal builder will coordinate the construction and any construction contractors you may need to engage for the project. A builder manages both suppliers and subcontractors.

On a standard building site there could be up to thirty people on-site, and the builder must know what each person is working on and have an understanding of how to undertake each subcontractor task so they know whether the contractor is producing quality work. A good builder must also be able to negotiate with and manage subcontractors to get the best outcome for the client.

Here is a list of the materials your builder might need to order from suppliers and the subcontractors they will manage on your home build:

Materials

- Appliances
- Blocks
- Bricks
- Carpet
- Cladding
- Concrete
- Door hardware
- Doors
- Light fittings
- Plumbing fittings
- Roof
- Roof and floor trusses
- Steel reinforcement
- Structural steel
- Tiles
- Timber
- Water tanks
- Window furnishings
- Windows

Subcontractors

- Blower door tester
- Bricklayers
- Carpenters
- Carpet layers
- Cleaners
- Concreters
- Concrete pumps
- Electricians
- Engineers
- Excavators
- Fencers
- Floor finishers
- Form workers
- Garage door installers
- Gas fitters
- Glaziers

- Heating ventilation and air conditioning installers
- Hydronic heating installers
- Joiners
- Landscapers
- Painters
- Phone/broadband installers
- Plasterers
- Plumbers
- Renderers
- Roofers
- Scaffolders
- Sheet metal workers
- Shower screen installers
- Solar installers
- Structural steel installers
- Termite treatment installers
- Tilers
- TV antenna installers
- Underground service locators
- Vinyl layers
- Waste water system installers
- Waterproofers
- Wood heater installers

When someone asks me if I am busy, subcontractors are usually the reason I say yes. There are thirty-eight subcontractors on this list and there are still more I haven't listed. Each subcontractor has questions for each home – and a builder will have multiple homes under construction at any one time. This is another great reason to have well developed and resolved building plans. If a detail exists only in the head of the architect/designer, builder or client, it may not make it to the right person on-site at the right time. A good builder will have an online project management system to communicate between all the different stakeholders in your building project.

Interior designer

The interior designer specifies all the fixtures, fittings and finishes inside and outside the house. They design tile layouts, joinery items and the home's colour palette and ensure each element comes together harmoniously. They will rearrange or design bathroom and kitchen layouts if needed. It's important to make interior design decisions early in the process to ensure the house is built according to the specifications and the budget doesn't blow out.

Landscape architect

Most people wait until after construction is finished to hire a landscape architect, but ideally you will have an idea of how you will manage the landscaping while you're designing your home to achieve a good connection between the building and the landscape. A landscape architect works with the area between the edges of the building and the edges of the block. They determine the placement of plantings, especially trees, as well as the footpaths, garden beds and driveways, and infrastructure such as pergolas, barbecue areas and fire pits.

Project manager

On most residential construction projects the builder becomes the project manager once the plans are handed over and the build begins. Sometimes the architect will project-manage the build, although some people hire an external project manager to help them to coordinate the job and ensure the builder and all the contractors are staying on track and following the plans. If the plans have been drawn up correctly and the builder has been involved through the design process, an external project manager shouldn't be necessary. This is where the implementation of the ABC Method can be cost saving and also result in better outcomes for you.

Broker, lender or financial advisor

It's a great idea to speak to someone about your building budget before you start the process. This then means you can work with a professional to determine your budget and lending capacity.

Finding your team

When you are looking for your architect/designer and builder, don't look just at the work they do, also look at *why* they do it. Companies that have a strong set of values and a clear 'why' will care more and deliver a better outcome than companies that don't.

Choosing your architect

Usually you will be attracted to an architect's site because of the images in their portfolio. You should then look for any testimonials on their site and check if you can speak to previous clients. When you're comparing architects, it can be a good idea to ask the same questions to ensure you can make an equal comparison.

What you are looking for is an architect who will listen to your unique needs, enabling you to feel understood and directed towards the best decisions. At the same time, you want an architect who is firm on the core design elements described in this book; they should know what works best for the building.

Investing in a quality architect

If I haven't made my point already, it is critically important to invest in good building design. In my experience, choosing the cheapest professional you can find is by far the most costly mistake people make when building a home. I have been to lots of new houses that have been built to high construction standards, with expert joinery and high-end fittings, but the design lets the house down. If the space has not been designed to suit the Six Elements of a Dream Home, the most expensive materials and best builder on the planet won't be able to make the building feel like home.

Decide whether you want a house or your dream home. Choosing an architect or building designer who can design a beautiful home, fine-tuned to your needs, is life-changing. Such a home has the power to make you feel recharged, healthier and happier and more connected with your family and friends. These are also the homes that win awards because the judges feel the authenticity of the design as they enter – the wow factor that goes beyond a great builder and good-quality materials.

Finding your builder

As with selecting an architect, when you're looking for a builder you should check their portfolio of work to see if they have experience in your style of build. Look for client testimonials and any awards they have won, and make sure they're a member of the Master Builders or Housing Industry Association, or the equivalent body in your country. Builders that are members of the Future Builder Society will also have access to the most relevant information and knowledge in the industry.

If possible, chat to previous clients and/or drive past some of their projects, both those completed and those under construction. Look for the quality of the craftsmanship and the state of the building site. Rubbish and mess everywhere are warning signs of disorganisation and poor safety standards. A builder who can't keep a clean site is a red flag and likely means they are not keeping an eye on all the fine details in your home either.

You will be spending the most time with your builder and their team through the project, so you must be on the same page and have a healthy partnership. Honesty and trustworthiness are important criteria for choosing a builder. You must be able to trust your builder and communicate easily. As one of my clients told me: 'You need to be able to trust and work with your builder. We were so fortunate to have had that. That's probably the most important aspect. With that, most problems go away.'

Investing in a quality builder

Often people base their selection of a builder on price alone, but just as it's worth investing in a good design, it's important to invest in a quality build.

Most builders I know aren't 100% focused on price and profit. The good builders are more focused on doing a good-quality job for their clients. This includes good customer service and communication, which is one of the best ways to avoid costly errors. When something goes wrong or off-track, because it will, you will have your building team there ready to step in and sort it out with you.

Questions to ask

There are a few specific questions you should ask your designer and your builder when you first make contact with them. You can have this page of the book open when you make the phone call and use these questions to structure your conversation. You can also find these in the Dream Home Journal at **www.lukedavies.co/dreamhomejournal**.

Questions to ask your architect

- What is your briefing process?
- How do you determine my design needs?
- What is your track record for meeting client budgets?
- Do you offer 3D walk-throughs?
- Do your rates include design consultants?
- Can you be involved in the construction phase?

Questions to ask your builder

- What is your track record for meeting client budgets?
- Have you won any awards?
- Do you have past clients we can talk to?
- How do you manage construction variations?

- What is the legal requirement for warranties on my home and what does it cover?
- What is the legal requirement for the defect period and what does it cover?
- What is the handover process for my home?
- How do you manage the construction schedule to guarantee the handover date?

If you are a builder reading this list, it is a good idea to have considered, legitimate answers to these questions. You may even need to fill a few gaps in your business so you can answer them.

Questions to ask yourself

- Do I have a good feeling about this architect or builder? You need to have a good relationship straight up.
- Do I feel they are honest?
- Do I feel they have a clear plan and are capable of following through my project to the end?

DREAM HOME-WORK

Research architects/designers and builders online and ask around for word-of-mouth recommendations.

When you are ready to start approaching architects and builders, ask them the same set of questions so you can compare them equally.

Summary

In this chapter we've reviewed the many different professional roles that go into a building project.

Depending on your build, you may not need all of these roles, but you will need the two most critical: the architect/designer and the builder. We've looked at what to look for in an architect and a builder and how to assess their skills.

12
Aligned Build Collaboration

Construction is an expensive business, and it's particularly difficult to gauge the price of building a unique architectural home. A one-size-fits-all square-metre rate is far too blunt an instrument to produce an accurate cost, as every detail and process must be costed separately, and the contribution of each specialist tradesperson must be factored into the quote. This process includes sourcing and totalling the cost of thousands of separate materials and tasks. Quoting on an average building project takes well over 200 hours just for one builder and their contractors.

In this chapter we'll look at the conventional method for undertaking this massive task, and the reasons why it fails to provide an accurate project cost. We'll then look at my solution to this problem: the ABC Method. This is a model where the builder, the architect and expert consultants work together from the start, which can have a hugely positive impact on your project, and your budget.

Conventional tendering

After deciding to do a custom-build, the first serious step most people take towards building their dream home is to engage an architect. They will then spend around a year first discussing their ideas then detailing a brief and working with the architect to develop plans for a home they love. Once the plans are drawn up, the architect may engage a quantity surveyor to provide a cost estimate on building the home.

The next step is to send the plans out to tender with builders. Most people approach between two and seven builders for a quote on their project. They provide each builder with the architectural plans, the engineering plans and the specifications, and then each builder submits a tender on building the house. Usually, builders have four to eight weeks from the first time they see the plans to provide a tender. The clients will then select a builder based on a number of factors, including the builder's portfolio of experience, the quality of their workmanship, the service standards and, most importantly, the price. Remember the lowest quote doesn't necessarily mean the lowest cost. Cost is more than just money, it's also time and benefits.

Unfortunately, many people are (unpleasantly) surprised by the price of their dream design. Although the clients may have the quantity surveyor's estimate as a ballpark figure, it's unusual for this figure to bear any resemblance to the tenders. This is because every builder has a different way of pricing and a different overhead structure, different subcontractor rates and different material rates. Even the builder's estimates are unlikely to be an accurate reflection of the final cost because, as we'll see in Chapter 13, the building estimate will inevitably include assumptions that frequently lead to budget blowouts.

Problems with conventional tendering

Architects often say the tendering process is a competitive system which allows market forces to deliver the best deal to their clients. This system, however, places all the responsibility on builders, who have not been involved in developing the plans, to cost the build. The competitive tendering process therefore means that builders often have a slim chance of winning a tender, so it's unlikely they will devote the passion and resources required to the estimating process. The result? Inaccurate building quotes. (One way around this is to pay builders for their tenders, which will give the builder an incentive to put resources into a more accurate quote, although the ideal way is to have them involved in the design.)

Imagine one set of house plans goes out to five builders for tender. To fully cost the build appropriately, they would typically spend 200 hours each on the tender, so that's 1,000 hours altogether. Each one of those builders would then engage about twenty subcontractors, who spend two hours each. Multiply this by five builders, that's another 200 hours. This means that costing just one set of plans and one version of that set takes up to 1,200 hours of resources and unpaid time, for a project that may never happen. Talk about waste and an inefficient use of time.

The architect is in a better position because they will be paid for the designs whether or not they're ever built. Don't worry – in many cases, architects truly are committed to assisting their clients and will do their best to adapt the designs to fit the budget once the plans are costed. This much is clear, though: if the tenders come in well above the client's budget, it can leave the architects in the awkward position of having to try to bring the plans back into the briefed budget.

Tendering processes have also become a bit sloppy and this allows builders to discreetly exclude a lot of costs, which makes them appear cheaper, but when you build, you realise they didn't include a lot of items and this results in variations. In most instances the project ends up costing more than expected, even with a fixed tender price.

Put simply, rarely in my career have I seen an architect-designed home developed through the conventional tendering process come in on budget.

The ABC Method

What comes first? Do you speak to an architect first and start your design or do you talk to a builder first for their thoughts about costs? The answer is both, teamwork makes the dream work, and you must speak to your architect and builder at the same time.

The architect and builder need to work together as a team from day one. We call it the ABC Method. It can also be called a negotiated tender and early contractor involvement (ECI) and is recognised as one way of mitigating the risks associated with tendering delivery models and increasing certainty around project deliverables and construction methodology. Under this system, the builder must agree to price the plans at specific stages in the design process, and the architect must agree to take the feedback from the builder onboard and feed it into the design. Some other key stakeholders – like engineers, a Passivhaus expert, window suppliers or joiners – may also need to be engaged early in the process.

The key elements of the ABC Method are:

- **Partnership on budget and brief:** The architect and the builder agree to work together to meet the budget and brief as a partnership.

- **Commitment to the client's best interests:** The architect and the builder agree to work with the owner's best interests in mind, and jointly commit to the outcome of finishing the home, rather than abandoning the project plans at some stage in the process.

- **Communication and allocation of responsibility:** The architect and the builder agree to a project schedule and an allocation of responsibilities. This includes a schedule of costings, reviews and staged meetings when the architect, builder and client will all come together.

The ABC Method fundamentally transforms how information flows in a building project. In conventional builds, as more people get involved – from the architect and builder to various subcontractors – the lines of communication don't just add up; they multiply exponentially. This creates a tangled web where critical details can easily get lost, misunderstood or simply not reach the right person at the right time. The following diagram visually demonstrates this escalating complexity.

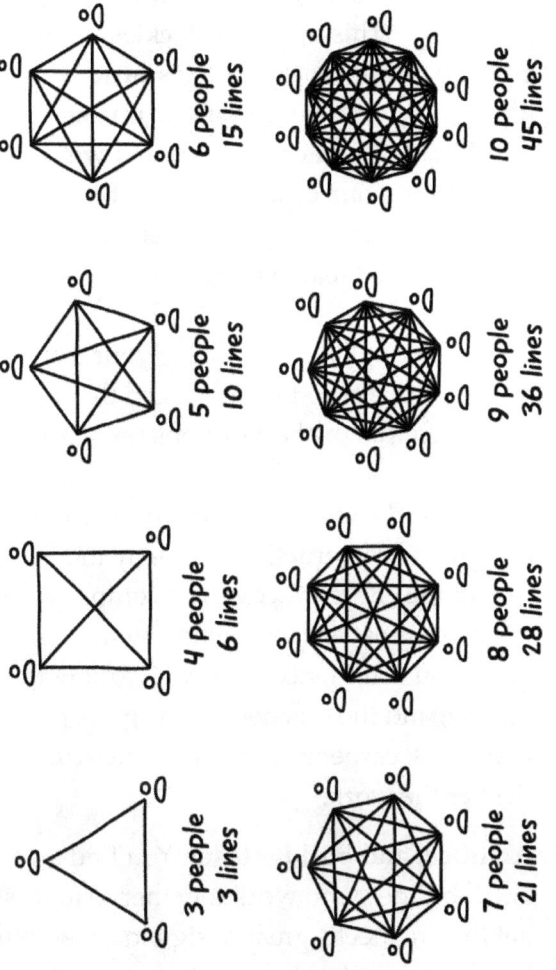

Communication patterns

This inherent complexity is precisely what the ABC Method is designed to overcome. By fostering direct collaboration and clear communication channels from the outset, the ABC Method ensures everyone is on the same page. This approach tackles the problem of multiplying communication lines head-on, minimising the risk of lost information, misinterpretations and costly delays. Later in this book, we'll introduce the BuildPrint, your central source of truth, which is essential for documenting all project information and ensuring a unified team effort.

There are a few options for putting your team together under the ABC Method. I have listed them in order of what I perceive as the best options respectively:

1. **Design and construct company:** You engage a design and construction company that can take care of the entire process. The company needs to have a great architect who listens to you and gives you confidence they will work within your budget, and the business needs great project managers, carpenters and subcontractors to deliver the work.

2. **Architect and builder team:** You find an architect and a builder who work together seamlessly. You get the architect's great design ideas with the builder's practical knowledge and costing data.

3. **Architect engages builder:** You appoint an architect and ask them to engage a builder for

the design process. You will most likely pay a fee to have the architect and builder work on this for you, but it's much better to get clear on the costings before you begin to design.

For option 1 you would sign a single agreement with the company; for option 2 and 3 you would sign a design proposal with the architect and an ECI agreement with the builder. Whatever you decide to do, unless you have an unlimited budget, don't get an architect to design your home without a builder's advice on the construction methods and the cost.

The other good thing about the ABC Method is that builders can't complain if the plans don't work, because they are part of the process from the start. If something doesn't work, it's the builder's responsibility to help pick it up in the design stage.

CASE STUDY: Conventional tendering versus ABC method

Let's compare stories from two recent clients, who both came to us with the same budget for their dream homes: AU$700,000.

Belinda and Dominic were a couple with a young family. They didn't have much flexibility to increase their budget, but they were clear on what they wanted and our architects worked with them through the Six

Elements process to design a home carefully tailored to their needs.

Our project manager costed the plans at two separate points in the design process to ensure the budget was on track, and the architects made adjustments to the plans in response. The design process took six months, and construction took another eight months – a total of fourteen months. The finished construction cost came in at AU$730,000, including design and approval fees and all site costs.

The other client, Scott, approached us with the same AU$700,000 budget, but with a completed set of plans. He'd worked with another architect for over eighteen months to develop them. To price Scott's plans, we had to ask a lot of questions so we could provide an accurate quote. We soon realised that his architect had not established some basic design parameters. For example, some of the selections and specifications were outdated and no longer available. For us to provide a price, Scott had to do a lot of extra work and decision-making. These considerations should have been made at the start of the design process. In the end Scott's estimate came in at AU$1,900,000, which was on top of the fees he'd paid to the architect.

Scott had been advised to use the conventional tendering system: he had engaged an architecture company to design his home, then taken the design to a minimum of three builders to get a quote comparison. The problem was that the plans could never have been used for a clear comparison between builders' quotes because they were missing vital information that required further input from the individual builders.

Scott was forced to cut off half his house and come up with another AU$250,000 to complete the build. In the end, we built Scott's home for AU$950,000 and he moved in three-and-a-half years after the design process began. Scott does love his home and he was lucky that he had the resources to extend his budget by 35% – but for many people this is simply not an option.

Some of the common mistakes I've seen in the conventional tendering process are:

- Going to a designer or architect who can't give you a total project budget and doesn't have any real-time building cost data
- Avoiding real conversations about budget and cost until the builders' quotes come in
- Approving plans that you can't visualise and then making changes during the build
- Taking advice and opinions from the wrong people, including friends, family and uneducated designers
- Deciding not to spend money on an architect, to free up more of the budget for construction

Designing a home is a complex project which requires professional training and experience.

DREAM HOME-WORK

If you're ready to embark on your dream home project, find out how your preferred architects and builders work with each other.

Ask questions about how and when projects will be costed and whether your favourite professionals would be open to working with the ABC Method.

Summary

In this chapter we've taken a close look at how the conventional tendering process works in the building industry and all the problems it causes. We've also looked at a better way to ensure a construction project stays on budget: the ABC Method.

By developing the ABC Method, I aim to change the way people think about building and encourage them to ask better questions when designing a home and picking a builder. At the end of the day, it's you, the homeowner, who has the power, as you make the final decisions about how to spend your money.

13
Budgeting Project Costs

The key to keeping a home building project on budget is to select and cost everything from the beginning of the project. This means every decision, from the roofing material to the tile selections, must be made right at the start during the design phase. Design and budget must work in parallel to keep the project on budget.

By now you should have a clear idea of the factors that go into a building's design. In this chapter we get down to brass tacks. We look at the difference between project cost and construction cost, the reasons why a one-size-fits-all square-metre rate is a blunt instrument for determining the cost of a build, the four components of determining the project cost, and the Four Ss that go into determining the home construction cost. We'll also take a look at more reasons why budgets on construction projects often blow out.

The myth of the square-metre rate

By far the most common question I'm asked when meeting new clients is 'What is the cost to build per square metre?' I am yet to meet a builder who can give an exact dollar amount answer for an architectural home build. It's the building equivalent of asking 'How long is a piece of string?' or 'How much is a bag of groceries?'

That's because there is no simple answer. The square-metre rate is affected by many factors, such as site slope, site access, soil conditions, ceiling heights, the shape of the house and the quality of finish. I've developed a home-construction-costing formula which takes these factors into account, called the Four Ss. The Four Ss offers a good approximation of the square-metre rate for the construction of a particular architectural home. Unfortunately, even this fairly accurate square-metre rate fails to take into account design consultants and project costs, so, naturally, comprehensive considerations need to be made.

Building square versus square metre

People often get confused between a building square and a building square metre. There is a big difference between the measurements. This is because it is a contest of imperial measurement versus metric measurement. For example, a building square is 10 feet by 10 feet, equalling 100 square feet. A building square metre is 1 metre by 1 metre. If you are used to talking in building squares, because you know your current house is 25 squares, you can convert that figure to square metres by multiplying it by 9.2903. Twenty-five squares multiplied by 9.2903 = 232.26 square metres. To convert square metres to squares, you can divide by 9.2903: 232.26 square metres divided by 9.2903 = 25 squares.

How to do a project feasibility study

A project's cost is made up of four components: architectural design, design consultants, site and external work and the home construction costs.

The home construction cost, in turn, can be broken down into four segments – the Four Ss: shape, style, selections and size.

The shape, style and materials selected are all dependent on your design decisions and they give you the estimated square-metre rate. The size simply indicates the overall area of your home; this is measured in square metres as well. Once you have determined the square-metre rate, you multiply this by the size, this is the square metres of the floor area to determine your home construction cost.

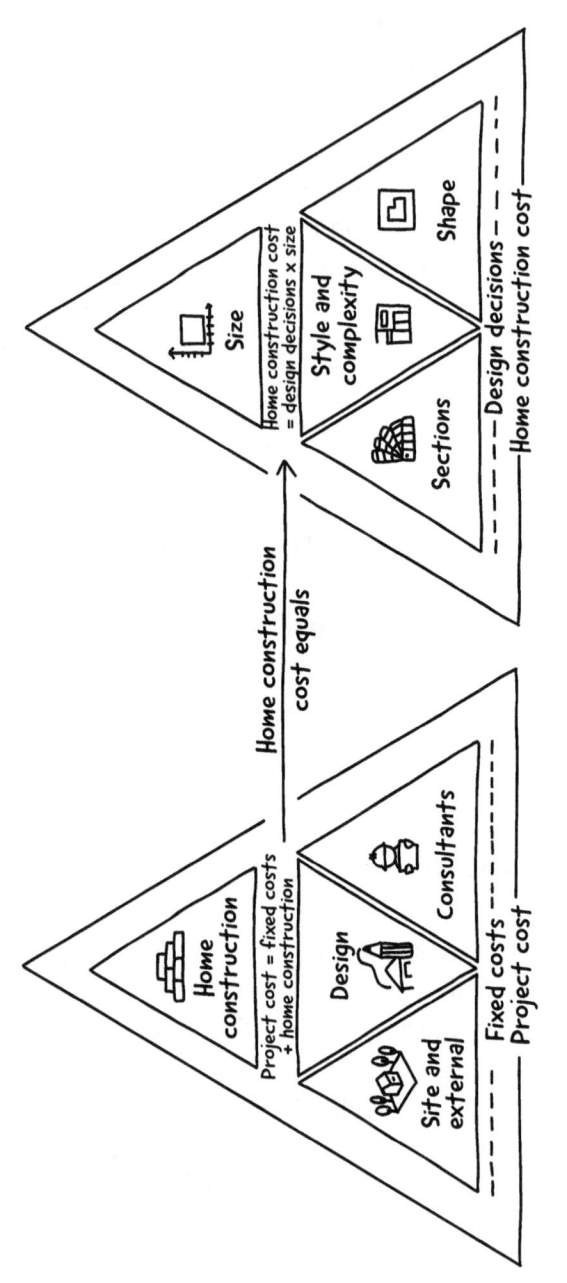

Project cost model

To make all this easier to understand, you can use the worksheet I use when calculating the project cost for a dream home – it's in the Dream Home Journal; you can download a copy at **www.lukedavies.co/dreamhomejournal**. Now let's take a look at each of these areas in detail.

Project costs

After you have purchased your land, the holistic project cost equation for building your home looks like this: holistic project = design + design consultants + site/external costs + house construction.

Architectural design

As we saw in Chapter 11, there are two options when it comes to designing your home. You can use a building designer or you can use an architect. One of the main differences between the two is time. An architect allows a lot more time to think, consider your home and resolve design decisions and details.

An architect has a high level of professional training. His or her role is to collect information from you (a brief) and use that information to design a building. Typically, an architect provides a creative response to your brief, bringing their experience and expertise into play.

A building designer has the credentials to design and draft building plans, but will usually provide less input at the conceptual level. He or she will draft up your own design ideas, rather than creatively interpreting the brief. You're likely to get a less adventurous and less technically complex design if you use a building designer.

No matter which option you choose, design fees are affected by the complexity and detail of the design. Two-storey houses, for example, are more complex to design and engineer than single-storey houses, as are homes designed for steep sites.

Design consultants

In Chapter 11 we also looked at the many different design consultants who may be required to contribute to your construction plans, depending on your individual situation.

Some design consultants will be accounted for in the fees for your architect/designer or builder, but you need to confirm this when you're contracting them. If the design consultants are not included, it's a good idea to ask your architect/designer or builder to recommend consultants – often they will have negotiated discounted rates that they can pass on to you. Also, it will work to your advantage if there's already a working relationship between the specialists: the builder and the architect/designer.

Design consultants' costs can vary widely and it's a good idea to obtain quotes for your real circumstances. You can use the table in the Dream Home Journal to gather your quotes.

Site and external work

These costs are specific to your site and project and will likely remain static even if you make changes to the building design.

In many cases, site and external costs will be included in your building contract; however, it's a good idea to split them out from your home construction cost. This will allow you to make adjustments to your home design and see how each change impacts on your project-specific square-metre rate.

Site and external costs include services connection, driveways, fencing, landscaping, water tanks, tree removal: anything outside your house.

- Driveway – gravel
- Driveway – concrete
- Storm water system
- Waste water system
- Power connection
- Gas connection
- Internet connection
- Water tanks
- Fire tank
- Shed
- Landscaping
- Fencing

- Decking
- Footpaths
- Removing trees
- Clothesline
- Mailbox

Home construction

Once I have an idea of the project cost, I like to discuss the construction cost as a separate topic. Most people think that architectural plans include all the details required to construct a building. This is not the case unless you've commissioned fully detailed plans (usually around 12% of the building cost). A lot of the information, such as material selections, is not included in the plans and is left up to the builder or the owner to select during construction. Every design decision has a cost implication. Making design decisions without knowing how they will affect the cost of your home is the number one killer of dream homes.

At my company we spend the required time on pricing each element of the build during the design phase. Our clients can then make informed decisions to adapt the design where needed before commencing the build. This is an intensive and timely process, but it is the best way to stay on budget. When we cost an external set of plans from another architect, our construction quotes are generally around twenty pages long. We provide itemised costs for each element and include the budget we've set aside for each decision that has not yet been made – these are called allowances.

This means there is clarity for the builders, but also clarity for the client. If you're over budget, you can see where there is potential to value manage or to cut costs. For example, you might decide to use differently sized windows, which will reduce the costs by AU$10,000. As you can see, though, if the windows are not separately itemised in the first place, there's no opportunity for you to have this kind of discussion with your team.

In the traditional process, builders have no idea of the real cost of a building project until they are contracted, because it's only then that they begin to get quotes on labour and materials. Generally, building contracts are signed with only 80% accurate information, leaving a 20% 'allowance' for provisional sums and prime costs.

Unfortunately, many builders supply a quote that is just one page with a single figure at the bottom and wording saying something like 'as per the plans.' This means there is no founding information for the client to make changes.

The Four Ss

This is the budgeting cost system I have developed. You can use it to work with your architect/designer and builder to obtain higher accuracy with

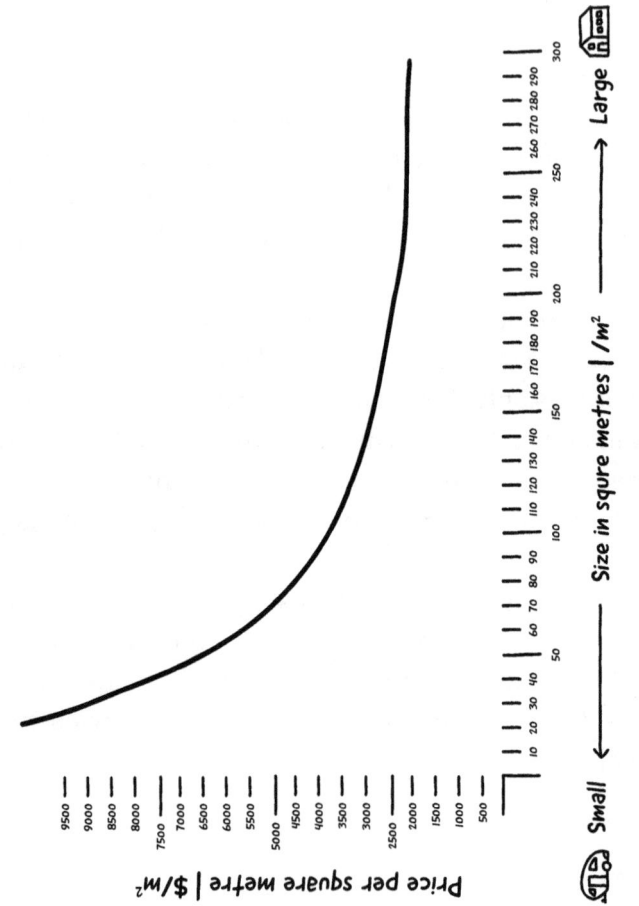

a square-metre rate for building your particular dream home.

The equation looks like this: home construction cost = (shape + style + selections) x size.

Size

You might think that the smaller your home, the cheaper it will be to build, but some costs are the same for all homes, irrespective of their size. For example, small and medium-sized homes still have a kitchen, bathroom, laundry and toilet. The plumber will charge about AU$20,000 to do the work based on fixtures (not square metres). A team of concreters can pour an 80-square-metre slab or a 110 square metre in a full day with the same labour costs. At a certain point it doesn't get any cheaper to build a smaller home. Size *does* make a big impact once you reach around 110 square metres, and square-metre rates begin to even out. This rate will differ according to the selections, style and shape of your home.

Selections

Selections are the materials and products you choose for your home. They include, for example, the flooring material, kitchen appliances and tapware.

I split selections into two categories to understand items and their cost, based not only on how they look and feel but also on how they affect the performance of the home. The first category is finishes, fittings and fixture-based selections like stone benchtops, tiles, paint, etc. The second is performance-based selections, such as windows and money spent on the building envelope (windows and external doors are usually the single biggest line item in terms of cost).

We aim to fully complete the decision-making process before the slab is poured. As you'll see below, the costs of making decisions during the construction process, known as build variations, can quickly add up.

Style and complexity

Style and complexity refers to the difficulty of building a given design. A simple design is obviously cheaper to build than a complex architectural design featuring, for example, raked ceilings, floor-to-ceiling windows and curving walls. The site can impact on the complexity, and some materials which may feature in complex designs, such as large steel beams or large roofing sheets, are difficult to transport.

Shape

The shape of the house has a large impact on the square-metre rate. If you look at the example, it becomes clear that two houses of the same size (based on square metres) would price up differently.

BUDGETING PROJECT COSTS

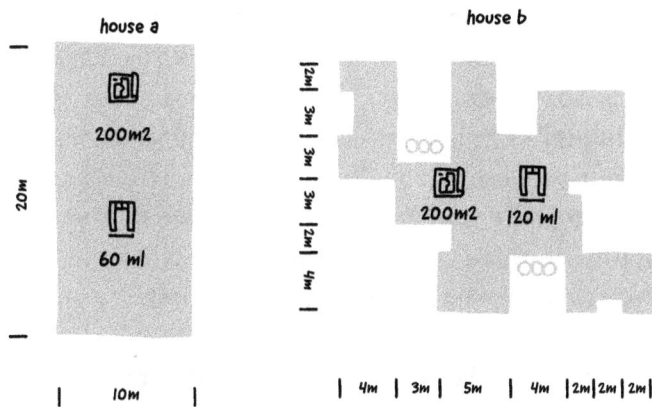

Shape versus cost

Build Component	House A	House B
Floor area – the same	200 m²	200 m²
Building perimeter (labour, timber, hardware)	60 lm	120 lm
External wall area (painting, cladding etc)	144 m²	288 m²
Internal wall area (plastering, insulation, painting)	144 m²	288 m²
External corners (labour, forming slab, framing, roofing, cladding)	4	20
Internal corners (labour, forming slab, framing, roofing, cladding)	0	16
Roof and truss design (labour, timber and hardware)	Simple	Complex
Foundation preparation (labour, excavation, steel reinforcement and concrete)	Simple	Complex
Cost per square metre (m²)	**$2,700**	**$3,700**

Both houses, A and B, are 200 square metres. The frame length in House A is 60 linear metres, while in House B it's 120 linear metres. The external wall area, which includes things like insulation, painting, cladding and labour, is 144 square metres in House A, while it's double that, at 288 square metres, in House B. The same figures apply to the internal wall area, which includes things like plastering, painting and labour.

There are also large differences in the number of corners – House A has four external corners, while House B has twenty external corners. This impacts on digging the footings, marking out the walls, framing and cladding. Meanwhile House A has no internal corners, while House B has sixteen internal corners.

All these factors impact on the square-metre rate, which works out at AU$2,700 per square metre for House A and AU$3,700 per square metre for House B, so $1,000 difference for the shape alone.

Counting costs

The most common reason building budgets blow out is build variations. These are changes to the plans that are made after construction has commenced.

When you sign a building contract, you commit to a set of plans which are the building's documentation. Any change to that agreement, whether it changes the cost or not, is a build variation. You should sign another, mini, variation contract every time you request a change, even one as small as the colour of a wall or moving a light switch, which varies the original contract. A good builder will have a strong process in place to manage variations – but many don't – and with each variation there's an opening for the cost and time to increase.

There are a number of reasons for build variations. Sometimes the clients haven't fully understood how the house will look; for example, they may want to move a window or change the joinery. This is a communication problem, solved by implementing tools like 3D walk-throughs and visualisations in the design process.

The most common reason for build variations is that design decisions have not yet been made. For example, construction on a building might start before the exact model of bath has been chosen. In this case, the estimator will leave an allowance in the project budget to cover the cost of the bath; however, it is disappointingly common for the allowance to be less than the final cost of the bath that is chosen.

Another reason for variations is that some decisions require changes to parts of the build that are already in place. For example, if you choose a bath with a plug in the centre but the slab was laid with a drainage hole at the end of the bath, the slab will need to be torn up, plumbing moved and the slab repoured to accommodate the central bath drainage.

Build variations can be stressful, expensive and time-consuming. Often, they lead to rushed decision-making to keep construction moving if the builder doesn't have a good process for variation management. My ideal build involves as few variations as possible or when there are variations to involve the architect as well as the client.

Allowances

There are two kinds of allowances: provisional sums and prime costs. A prime cost covers the materials only, while a provisional sum covers both the materials and the labour.

For example, if you have an allowance in your plans of AU$100 per square metre for tiling your bathroom, it's important to check if this is a provisional sum or a prime cost. If it's a prime cost, you can buy tiles that cost AU$100 per square metre and stay within your budget; if it's a provisional sum, you must factor in the cost of the tiler to lay each metre of tiles and include this in your AU$100 per metre.

You aim to reduce the amount of allowances in your building contract, as they represent a lot of additional work and the potential for miscommunication.

Cost of build variations

In my businesses, our D&C process is used to make most design decisions before building starts, which means there are few variations, but we do also build designs created by outside architects. Below is some of our data showing the typical cost difference between building from a set of plans designed by an outside architect and an inhouse D&C process where we are involved from the start and use the ABC Method.

Project	Method	Building contract	Build variations	Final cost
Home 1	Build	AU$600,000	51	AU$1,600,000
Home 2	Build	AU$900,000	72	AU$1,500,000
Home 3	Build	AU$500,000	38	AU$880,000
Home 4	D&C	AU$750,000	3	AU$740,000
Home 5	D&C	AU$950,000	7	AU$980,000
Home 6	D&C	AU$400,000	1	AU$410,000

As you can see, costing a build is an enormous process involving thousands of small calculations and, of course, these calculations change every time there's a change to the design.

Using a D&C process means you are more likely to hit the brief and the budget, rather than missing the brief, going over the budget and going over time.

There are many myths about costing a building; here are just a few:

- Plans aren't that important – you can save money on drawing plans and spend more on the build.
- Building quotes from different builders can be compared based on a simple square-metre rate.
- Builders' quotes are all the same, and can be compared like-for-like based on the plans.
- Home owners can skip the architect and take care of the design process themselves, then take the plans to a builder to quote.

DREAM HOME-WORK

Grab a piece of paper and write these four headings:

1. Architect/designer
2. Design consultants
3. Site and external
4. Home construction

Now list the items in each category that you will need for your project and estimate a cost for each item. You can use the Four Ss system to try to get an idea of your individual square-metre rate for your home construction. You should then tally up the total to get your project feasibility number. You can get a project feasibility template in the Dream Home Journal.

Are you now ready to build your dream home? Do the Ready to Build Quiz at www.lukedavies.co/readytobuildquiz.

Summary

In this chapter we've had a look at the many factors that feed into costing a build and the reasons why providing an accurate square-metre rate is an impossible task if there is a lack of information about the external site costs and design consultant costs, the size, selections, style, and the shape of the home. We've also seen how build variations, caused by leaving design decisions to the construction phase, can contribute to exponential cost increases.

Despite this, many people choose a builder based largely on the square-metre rate they provide, only to find that their budgets blow out almost as soon as construction begins. A better way is to put time into the pre-construction planning and make as many design decisions, and cost them, before construction begins.

14
The Aligned Dream Home

You want to build your dream home but *where do you start*? The issues we've looked at through Part III of this book can cause huge problems and miscommunications in the construction industry, which lead to budget blowouts and delays. The good news is, there are ways to avoid them.

In this chapter I'll introduce the system my company uses to dodge these bullets. We'll look at the keystone of our model which links the design and construction phases: the BuildPrint. I'll also run through our design process, how we develop our costings and the key project milestones we hit. It's a process that can be implemented for any home construction build. You might decide to use it as a template for your own project.

The BuildPrint

The BuildPrint is the foundation of all of our projects. It's comparable to a building plan set or blueprint, but we use the term BuildPrint because our plans include more than just the minimum to get a building approval – they contain resolved ideas and the detail the builder needs to communicate the ideas into a physical form and construct the home. In other words, there are minimal allowances because most of the design decisions have been made and are detailed in the BuildPrint, so everyone is *on the same page*.

The BuildPrint marks the culmination of our design process – from this point the project transitions from design into construction. How do we develop the BuildPrint? Let's take a look at the Aligned Dream Home design process.

The home design phase takes around twelve months. I recommend to plan slowly so you can build fast, resolving as many of the questions as possible while the dream home is still 'on paper'. Our design process is divided into five phases, as below:

- **Sketch design + project feasibility**
  During the feasibility phase our architect and builder meet with the client and establish the ABC model. During the meeting, either at our offices or on the client's land (if it's purchased), we discuss the process, costs and site-specific

ideas and conduct a site audit for the buildability, sketch design and feasibility study.

- **Concept design + design development**
  Our briefing process continues with a conversation and a list of questions that when answered will form the design brief, which is a written description of your concept plans. The team discusses the design needs and budget, drawing on any images, mood boards or ideas the client has gathered, and turn these into sketch designs. Towards the end of Stage 1, a concept design, 3D walk-through and cost estimate is presented to the client. The client's revisions and changes are incorporated before the concept design and budget estimate is approved by the client.

- **Planning/development application + interior design**
  In this phase clients work with our interior designer on selections like the colour palette, cabinetry layouts, tiling, appliances, flooring, kitchen and bathroom fittings, fixtures and finishes. We present an interiors proposal and cost estimate to the client around midway through this stage, then spend a few weeks incorporating revisions and changes until the interiors can be approved by the client. During this phase we also handle development approvals, including any required design consultant reports that haven't been done in Stage 1, such as a soil and

site classification report, waste water design and bushfire assessments.

- **Construction documentation**
  In this phase, with the concept design and interiors signed off, we develop the final BuildPrint. This is the central source of truth for the home design. We liaise with contractors, building suppliers, energy rating consultants, building surveyors, certifiers and engineers to develop a set of design documents with all selections included. We also submit building approval applications to local authorities.

- **Construction support**
  In this phase, we help with questions throughout the construction, including schedule, budget, quality, communication, construction details, material selection and issue resolution. By keeping the architect involved in these areas, we ensure the challenges that arise can be discussed in the ABC Method and the end result meets quality standards, ultimately leading to a successful and satisfying project outcome. Depending on the type of contract, we also take care of contract administration.

Once the BuildPrint is signed off, construction can begin and usually takes a further eight to eighteen months.

Advantages of the BuildPrint plans include:

- **Site-specific costing:** With a large percentage of details resolved early in the process, the builder can give a fixed-price contract with no or a low amount of allowances.

- **Written confirmation:** We use the return brief as written confirmation of everything our clients have told our team and it forms the basis for every stage of the process. Many people will be a part of the design and construction process; without this no one will have context and your dream home narrative will be lost or diluted along the way.

- **Accurate timelines:** We provide detailed schedules to capture the anticipated program and timelines.

- **On-track budgets:** With an accurate design brief and budget, keeping your project on budget is easier. Even if the project evolves, which is part of the beauty of an architectural home, the brief and budget can be updated and cross-referenced at each stage.

Project milestones

There are five main milestones or sign-off points: design proposal and ECI agreement, project feasibility, design brief, Buildprint, building contract handover.

1. **Design proposal and ECI agreement:** The architect will provide a design proposal and reference the project feasibility. The builder will provide an ECI agreement. If both are within the same company, these could be combined.
2. **Design brief:** This is a detailed description of what your home will be like and forms the basis of the information for your architect.
3. **Building plans (BuildPrint):** This has been achieved once the construction plans have been completed and are ready for the final contract price.
4. **Building contract:** Before the building work starts you need a clear construction contract with minimal or no provisional sums or prime costs (allowances).
5. **Handover:** This is the final stage when you sign off you are happy with your home and get the keys to move in.

Things may change at any stage of design, of course, and they always do as the ideas come to life. It's important, however, to keep a record of all changes and their impacts on the budget. Architect, builder and clients must sign a revised design brief and budget whenever changes are made.

The brief remains a pivotal document throughout the design process and continues to be crucial through the construction process. At every stage in the process, whenever decisions are being made, my company loops back to make sure we are still meeting all critical elements in the updated brief, including the budget.

Accurate costings

We start pricing from the feasibility stage so we know that our costing information is approximately 70% accurate before we even start the design. As we move through the design development, we continue to increase our accuracy until we know that our pricing is 95% to 100% accurate when we produce the BuildPrint.

Clear timelines

A Gantt chart or schdule is a visual view of each critical step in a process, the actions required, people responsible and how each step relates to the next. Our Gantt charts give our clients a snapshot view of when to expect building to start and when they will be able to move into their dream home. We provide separate Gantt charts for the design process (brief to BuildPrint) and the construction process (building contract to move-in date).

While the Gantt chart will often need to be adapted due to weather or other factors, it's a vital tool for everyone working on the project to understand progress. If your architect or builder cannot provide a simple schedule or Gantt chart, even if it's an example, this should be a warning sign that they don't have a good system for managing their internal process or delivering on time.

Communication

Constructing a home is an enormous project involving dozens of people and requiring many lines of information transfer that can break down at any link in the chain. Only with clear documentation – such as the BuildPrint, clear project timelines, visualisation tools such as 3D modelling and online project management tools – can you be certain everyone is on the same page.

3D modelling and digital twins

The more you can make it visual, the better. The traditional paper plans you see are 2D plans and they are an important part of construction. They are essential for documenting and engineering concepts, gaining approvals and working with accurate measurements; however, 2D plans are not a great way to communicate 3D ideas.

A 3D model helps your brain absorb the design, it helps the architect visualise the design, and it helps the builder and contractors understand how to estimate the design. It's easier to pick colour and selections when you can try them in the 3D modelling. It's easier to pick up on errors in the design stages before building starts. Using a 3D model clarifies the communication and helps the builders on-site to understand the plans, rather than flicking through hundreds of pages of 2D plans.

I've known of people who are building multi-million-dollar homes and trying to understand and visualise their designs using only 2D plans. They don't know what they're getting or what it's going to look and feel like. Once the client sees a 3D model, everything changes – seeing is feeling and they can *feel* the space. These days, 3D modelling is advanced – for example, you can click around inside a geolocated model and look at your views through the virtual windows, feel how much space you'll have in the bathrooms and see the paint colours on the walls. Some clients even like to use a virtual reality headset to walk around the space.

For my business, 3D modelling is an essential part of the design and client communication process. We upload the plans and the client can view them in 3D using an app on their phones. Each time their plan is updated, they can view the new 3D models on their phone, show their friends and give us feedback.

DREAM HOME-WORK

> If you're already working with a team to design your dream home, discuss using the Aligned Dream Home system to increase the communication and transparency on your project.

Summary

The three main issues for most building projects are running over time, running over budget and not getting the benefits expected from a new build. My solution is the Aligned Dream Home, designed to incorporate the Six Elements through a transparent and clear four-step process, the ABC Method, with architect, builder and client all working together with the BuildPrint as the outcome. This process aligns you with your team, it aligns your vision with the design, it aligns the building with the site, and it aligns the design brief with the budget.

Conclusion

Throughout the course of this book, I've shared the secrets of the processes my company uses to build dream homes.

If you set a clear goal, find the right team and use these tools, you too can achieve a dream home that's a perfect fit for your lifestyle and needs, built on time and on budget. Not only that, but the whole journey will be a pleasurable experience that is joyful and inspiring.

Using the Six Elements process will provide you with a deep understanding of your needs, encouraging you to evaluate all aspects of your life and how they impact on your design. Additionally, by bringing the right team together from the start, you can reduce the miscommunication, poor decision-making and confusion that is the cause of most wasted time, budget and benefits on architectural home builds.

I've provided you with clear information on all the elements that need to come together for a home building project, including the specialists and professionals you'll need to consult at both the design and construction stage, and costing information that can inform your decisions at every point in the process.

Wherever you are on your journey, please remember that you can access our Dream Home Evaluation – a fun, free quiz that evaluates your current home, or home plans, against the Six Elements. Find it on our website: **www.lukedavies.co**. You'll find many more resources on our site to help plan your home design. It includes the Dream Home Journal, articles, case studies, and you can connect with us for more resources, including workshops, courses and guides, to fuel your home design journey.

I've unpacked and demystified the process and removed the sense of overwhelm that many people feel in contemplating taking this step. My hope is that, equipped with this information, you feel empowered to take the brave and inspirational step of building the home of your dreams.

One thing I can promise you is that you will be glad you took the decision to custom-build your dream home.

CONCLUSION

Nothing beats the feeling of living in your personal sanctuary. I can attest to the satisfaction and pride you feel as you drive up to your home after a long day away. When you step across the threshold, all the stresses of the world seem to lift from your shoulders. Here is the place that holds space for everything you value, supports your health and provides a sense of wellbeing and fulfilment that cannot be gained from anything else. Your dream home.

Notes

1. The Six Elements of a Dream Home is a registered trademark.
2. Australian Government Department of Climate Change, Energy, the Environment and Water, 'Indoor air' (10 October 2021), www.dcceew.gov.au/environment/protection/air-quality/indoor-air, accessed 18 April 2024
3. The Habitat Hierarchy is a registered trademark.
4. AH Maslow, 'A Theory of Human Motivation', *Psychological Review*, 50 (1943), 370–396, https://psycnet.apa.org/record/1943-03751-001, accessed 2 December 2024
5. Tasmanian Government, 'The List' (9 December 2021), www.thelist.tas.gov.au/app/content/home, accessed 18 April 2024
6. J Clear, *Atomic Habits* (Random House, 2018)

7 CommSec, *Australian Houses are World's Biggest: CommSec home size trends report* (6 November 2020), www.commbank.com.au/articles/newsroom/2020/11/commsec-home-size-trends-report, accessed 23 April 2024

8 Livable Housing Australia, 'Livable housing design guidelines' (no date), https://livablehousingaustralia.org.au/design-guidelines, accessed 18 April 2024

9 National Disability Insurance Scheme, 'Specialist disability accommodation' (5 August 2022), https://ourguidelines.ndis.gov.au/supports-you-can-access-menu/home-and-living-supports/specialist-disability-accommodation, accessed 18 April 2024

10 M Jimenez et al, 'Associations between nature exposure and health: a review of the evidence', *International Journal of Environmental Research and Public Health*, 18/9 (2021), 4790, https://doi.org/10.3390/ijerph18094790

11 M Triguero-Mas et al, 'The effect of randomised exposure to different types of natural outdoor environments compared to exposure to an urban environment on people with indications of psychological distress in Catalonia' (PLOS ONE, 2017), https://doi.org/10.1371/journal.pone.0172200

12 D Li et al, 'Epigenetic regulation of gene expression in response to environmental exposures: from bench to model', *Science of the Total Environment*, 776 (1 July 2021), https://doi.org/10.1016/j.scitotenv.2021.145998

13 C Mathews, 'What is Building Biology?', Healthy Homes Advisor (no date), www.healthyhomeadvisor.com/what-is-building-biology, accessed 8 November 2024

14 Australian Government Department of Climate Change, Energy, the Environment and Water, 'Indoor air' (10 October 2021), www.dcceew.gov.au/environment/protection/air-quality/indoor-air, accessed 18 April 2024

15 J Douwes, W Eduard, PS Thorne, 'Bioaerosols', *International Encyclopedia of Public Health* (2nd edn, Academic Press, 2017), 210–218

16 C Campanale et al, 'A detailed review study on potential effects of microplastics and additives of concern on human health', *International Journal of Environmental Research and Public Health*, 17/4 (13 February 2020), https://doi.org/10.3390/ijerph17041212

17 Ibid

18 Dr M Dewsbury et al, *Scoping Study of Condensation in Residential Buildings* (Australian Building Codes Board, 23 September 2016), www.abcb.gov.au/sites/default/files/resources/2022/Scoping-study-of-condensation-residential-buildings.pdf, accessed 23 April 2024

19 SK Brown, 'Beating the $12 billion cost of polluted air' (Commonwealth Scientific and Industrial Research Organisation Press Release, ref 98/55, 1998)

20 United States Environmental Protection Agency, 'Carbon monoxide's impact on indoor air

quality' (25 September 2023), www.epa.gov/indoor-air-quality-iaq/carbon-monoxides-impact-indoor-air-quality, accessed 23 April 2024

21 United States Environmental Protection Agency, 'Volatile organic compounds' impact on indoor air quality' (15 August 2023), www.epa.gov/indoor-air-quality-iaq/volatile-organic-compounds-impact-indoor-air-quality, accessed 23 April 2024

22 United States Environmental Protection Agency, 'Interactive tour of the indoor air quality demo house' (19 August 2023), www.epa.gov/indoor-air-quality-iaq/interactive-tour-indoor-air-quality-demo-house, accessed 23 April 2024

23 World Health Organization, 'High indoor temperatures', in *WHO Housing and Health Guidelines* (National Library of Medicine, 2018), www.ncbi.nlm.nih.gov/books/NBK535285, accessed 23 April 2024

24 World Health Organization, 'Low indoor temperatures and insulation', in *WHO Housing and Health Guidelines* (National Library of Medicine, 2018), www.ncbi.nlm.nih.gov/books/NBK535294, accessed 23 April 2024

25 Health and Safety Executive, *How to Deal with Sick Building Syndrome* (3rd edn, 2000), www.hse.gov.uk/pubns/priced/hsg132.pdf, accessed 23 April 2024

26 L Villazon, 'Can I get sunburnt through glass?', *Science Focus* (no date), www.sciencefocus.com/science/can-i-get-sunburnt-through-glass, accessed 23 April 2024

27 ML Pall, 'Wi-Fi is an important threat to human health', *Environmental Research*, 164 (2018), 405–416, https://pubmed.ncbi.nlm.nih.gov/29573716, accessed 2 December 2024
28 AE van den Berg et al, 'Green space as a buffer between stressful life events and health', *Social Science & Medicine*, 70/8 (2010), https://pubmed.ncbi.nlm.nih.gov/20163905, accessed 2 December 2024
29 Harvard Medical School, 'Sour mood getting you down? Get back to nature' (Harvard Health Publishing, 30 March 2021), www.health.harvard.edu/mind-and-mood/sour-mood-getting-you-down-get-back-to-nature, accessed 23 April 2024
30 Division of Sleep Medicine, 'Why sleep matters: consequences of sleep deficiency' (Harvard Medical School, 1 October 2021), https://sleep.hms.harvard.edu/education-training/public-education/sleep-and-health-education-program/sleep-health-education-45, accessed 23 April 2024
31 Division of Sleep Medicine, 'Sleep and disease risk' (Harvard Medical School, 1 October 2021), https://sleep.hms.harvard.edu/education-training/public-education/sleep-and-health-education-program/sleep-health-education-45, accessed 23 April 2024
32 Health Direct, 'Insomnia' (September 2023), www.healthdirect.gov.au/insomnia, accessed 23 April 2024

33 National Health Service, 'Sleep and tiredness' (no date), www.nhs.uk/live-well/sleep-and-tiredness, accessed 23 April 2024

34 Harvard Medical School, 'Blue light has a dark side' (Harvard Health Publishing, 7 July 2020), www.health.harvard.edu/staying-healthy/blue-light-has-a-dark-side, accessed 23 April 2024

35 WUFI is a registered trademark.

36 D Walzer et al, 'Effects of home particulate air filtration on blood pressure: a systematic review', *Hypertension*, 76/1 (2020), 44–50, https://doi.org/10.1161/HYPERTENSIONAHA.119.14456

37 Passivhaus Institut: https://passiv.de, accessed 19 April 2024

38 Adapted from O Young and W Steffen, 'The Earth System: Sustaining Planetary Life-Support Systems', *Principals of Ecosystem Stewardship* (2009), https://link.springer.com/chapter/10.1007/978-0-387-73033-2_14, accessed 8 November 2024

39 D Attenborough, *A Life on Our Planet* (Ebury Press, 2022)

40 PJ Crutzen and EF Stoermer, 'The Anthropocene', *Global Change Newsletter*, 41 (2000), 17–18, www.igbp.net/download/18.316f18321323470177580001401/1376383088452/NL41.pdf, accessed 2 December 2024

41 PJC Steffen, 'How long have we been in the Anthropocene era?', *Climatic Change*, 61/3 (2003), 251, https://link.springer.com/article/10.1023/B:CLIM.0000004708.74871.62, accessed 2 December 2024

42 S Whitmee et al, 'Safeguarding Human Health in the Anthropocene Epoch: Report of the Rockefeller Foundation–Lancet Commission on planetary health', *The Lancet*, 386/10007 (2015), 1973–2028, www.thelancet.com/article/S0140-6736(15)60901-1/fulltext, accessed 2 December 2024

43 M Romanello et al, 'The 2023 Report of the Lancet Countdown on Health and Climate Change: The imperative for a health-centred response in a world facing irreversible harms', *The Lancet*, 402/10419 (2023), 2346–2394, www.thelancet.com/journals/lancet/article/PIIS0140-6736(23)01859-7, accessed 2 December 2024

44 K Dolan, 'How To Solve Climate Change: Bill Gates Wants You To Know Two Numbers', *Forbes* (14 February 2021), www.forbes.com/sites/kerryadolan/2021/02/14/how-to-solve-climate-change-bill-gates-wants-you-to-know-two-numbers/?sh=67e4239b531f, accessed 16 May 2024

45 J Gergis, *Humanity's Moment* (Island Press, 2023)

46 BSI, 'Insight from the Built Environment's journey to net zero', BSI Net Zero Week webinars (2021), www.bsigroup.com/globalassets/documents/bsol/the-built-environments-journey-to-net-zero.pdf, accessed 8 November 2024

47 X Wang, D Chen and Z Ren, 'Assessment of climate change impact on residential building heating and cooling energy demand in Australia', *Building and Environment*, 45/7 (July 2010), 1663–1682, https://doi.org/10.1016/j.buildenv.2010.01.022

Acknowledgements

This book wouldn't exist without the support and contributions of many incredible people. I extend my deepest gratitude to:

My Family

To my amazing wife, Janenna Davies, thank you for your unwavering love, patience and belief in me. Your support has been my constant source of strength and inspiration.

To my wonderful parents, Peta and Quentin Davies, thank you for instilling in me the values of hard work, perseverance and a love for creating with my hands.

To my brothers, Andrew and Liam Davies, thank you for your unwavering support and for always believing in my crazy ideas, even when they seemed impossible.

To my sister-in-law, Catelyn (Wig) Richards, thank you for your encouragement and for always being there to lend an ear and offer a fresh perspective.

Colleagues and friends

To Mitch Emery, Michael Loubser, Chris Gilbert, John Harris, Glen Carlson, Scott Stewart and Clarence Macalister, thank you for your invaluable insights, inspiring conversations and support. Your friendship and belief in this project have been instrumental in its completion.

Writers and editors

To Monique Perrin, Alison Fraser, Eve Makepeace and Anke Ueberberg, thank you for your exceptional talent and dedication in helping me bring this book to life. Your expertise in crafting compelling narratives and refining my ideas has been invaluable.

And to everyone else who has contributed to this book, thank you from the bottom of my heart.

The Author

Luke Davies is a passionate entrepreneur and builder who embodies The Art of Building as a way of life in every aspect of his existence. He believes that anything can be built when you set your intention, whether it's a dream home, a thriving business or a fulfilling life. Applying a philosophy of maximising value and relentlessly eliminating waste, he uses these principles across all his ventures, including Davies Construction, Align Architecture and Future Builder Co.

As a licensed builder and certified Passivhaus tradesperson, Luke is recognised for his commitment to quality, innovation and sustainability. His expertise extends beyond building homes; he is a sought-after consultant, coach and mentor, sharing his expertise with other builders and businesses to help them thrive.

When not immersed in his work, Luke cherishes time with his wife, Janenna, and their two children, Bella and Roy. An avid outdoorsman, he finds joy in camping, hiking and exploring the natural beauty of Tasmania and beyond.

🌐 www.lukedavies.co

www.ingramcontent.com/pod-product-compliance
Lightning Source LLC
Chambersburg PA
CBHW050639170426
43200CB00008B/1088